PRINTED IN EUROPE

1 CITÉ RIVERIN
75010 PARIS
www.disvoir.com

ISBN 978-2-914563-52-9

Text attributions:

10-15:	CARSON MCCULLERS
18-19:	LEAH SINGER
34-35, 40-41, 45:	LEE RANALDO
54-59:	ROBERT SMITHSON

Audio CD 136915 zagzig003 /1 © LEAH SINGER & LEE RANALDO

The sound piece, *WATER DAYS / JOURS D'EAU*, was commissioned by the Atelier de Création Radiophonique (ACR) de France Culture, and produced by the Centre National des Arts Plastiques (CNAP) and the Ministère de la Culture, as part of a public commission. It was broadcast on April 26, 2009. www.franceculture.com

WATER DAYS

LEAH SINGER • LEE RANALDO

Series ZAGZIG

directed by

PHILIPPE LANGLOIS & FRANK SMITH

In the same Series

Laurie Anderson: *Nothing in my Pockets*

Jonas Mekas: *To Petrarca*

Ryoji Ikeda: *Dataphonics*

Water Days

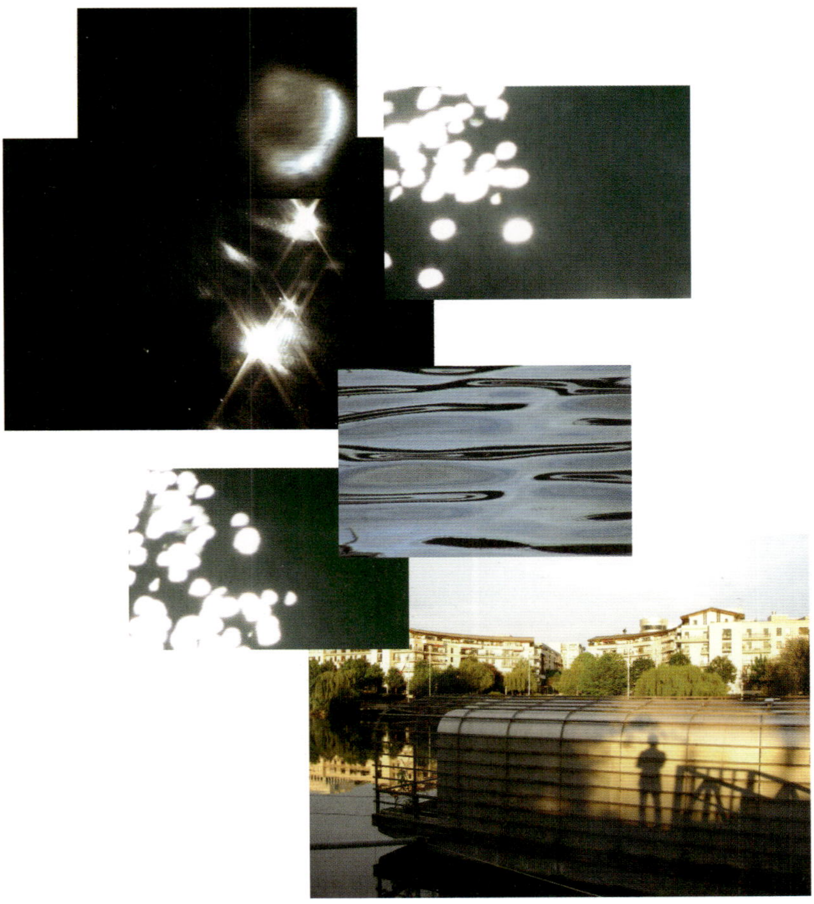

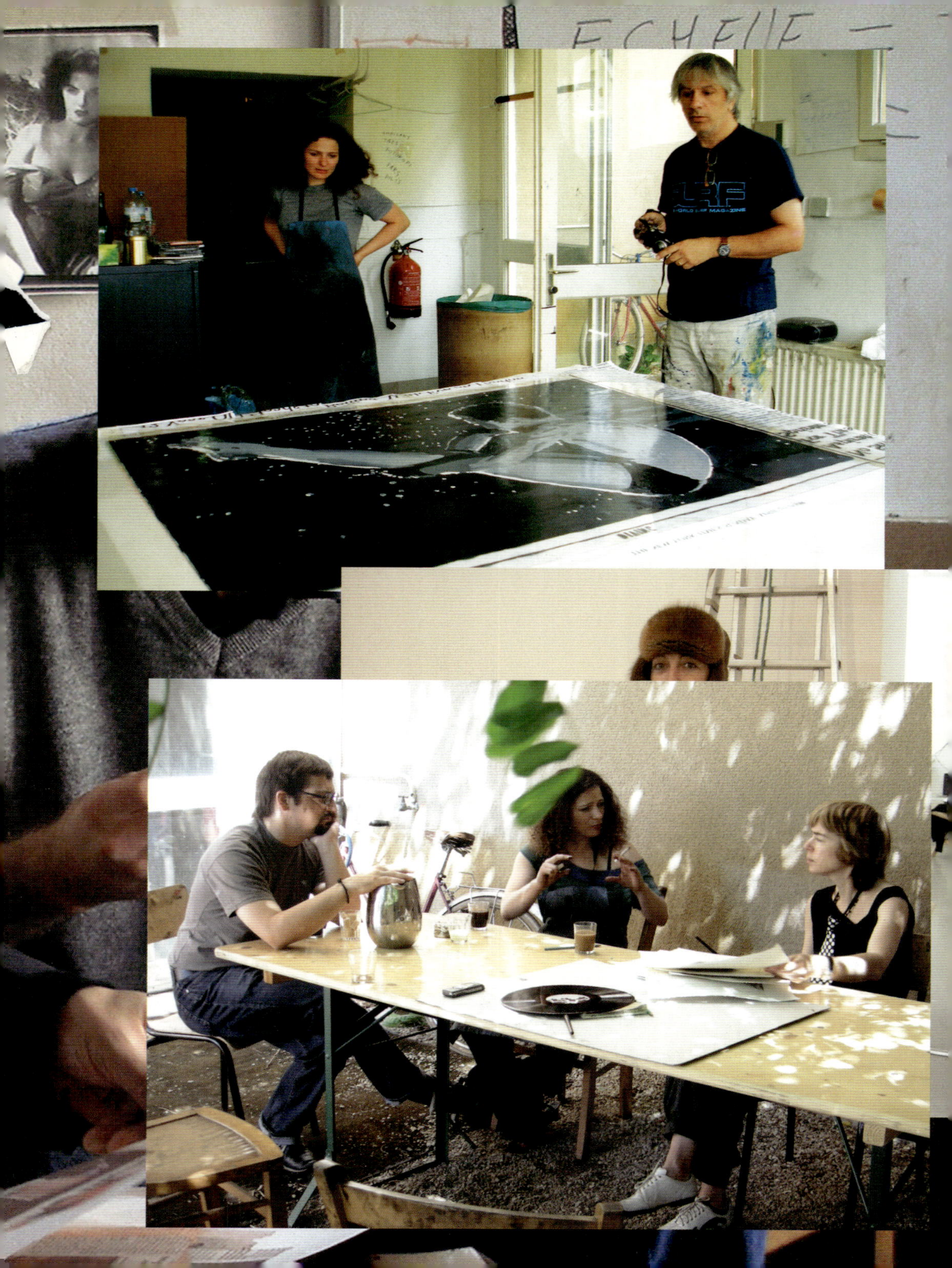

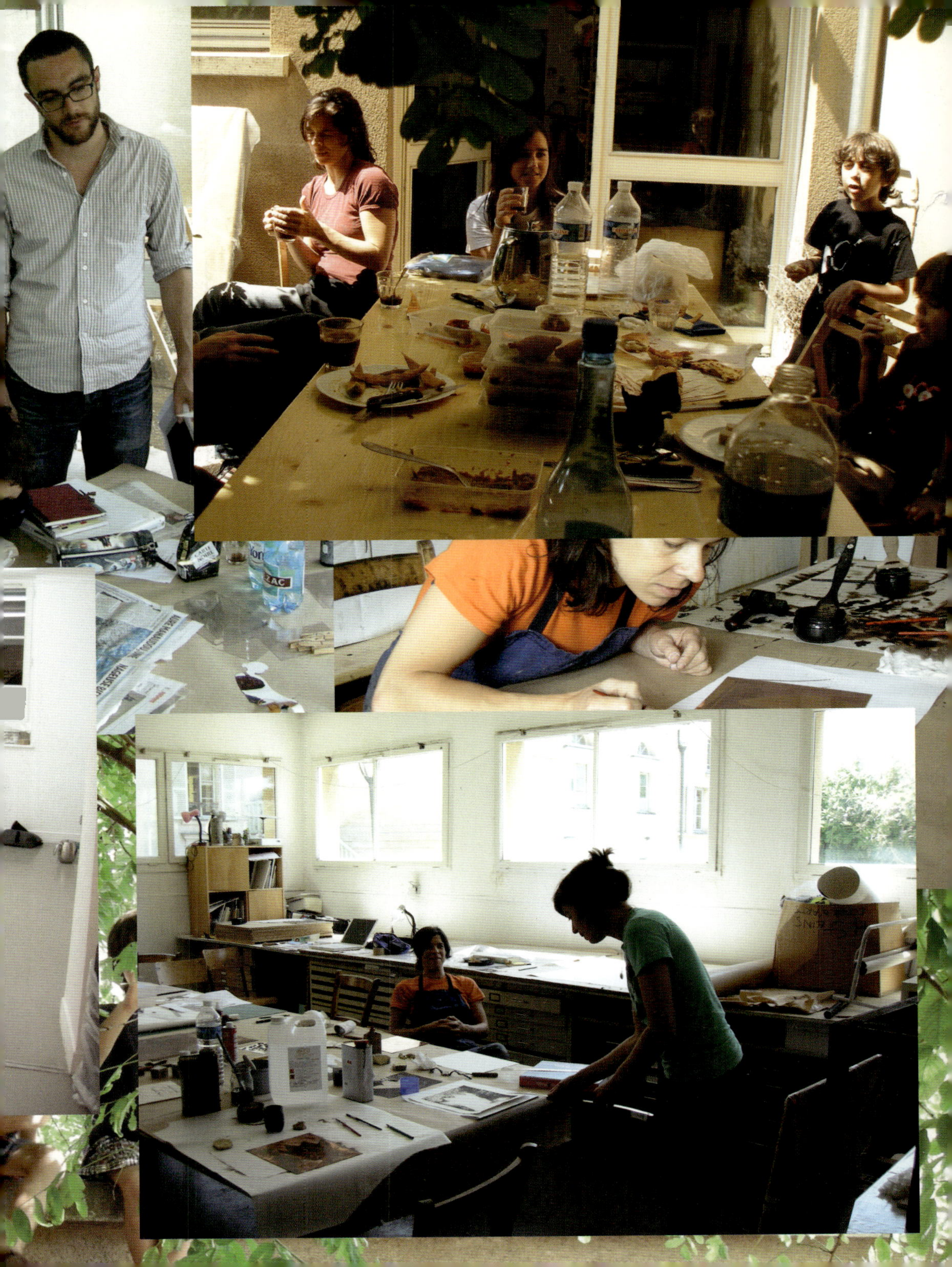

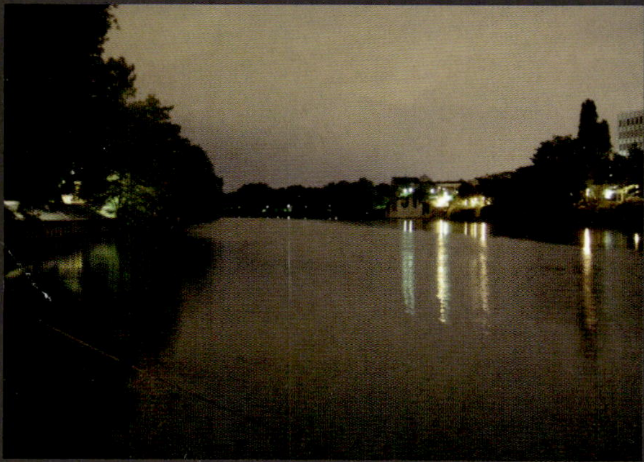

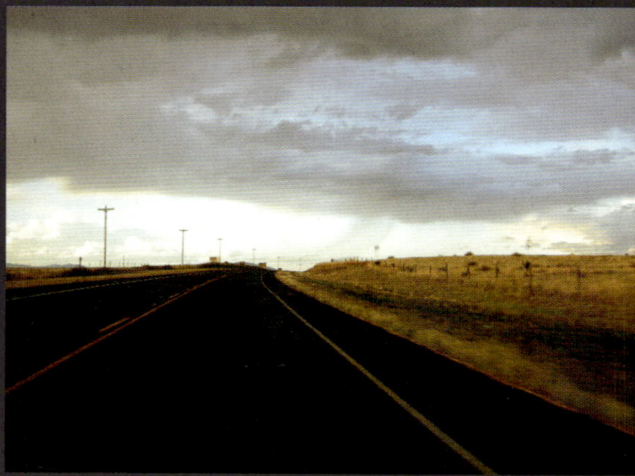

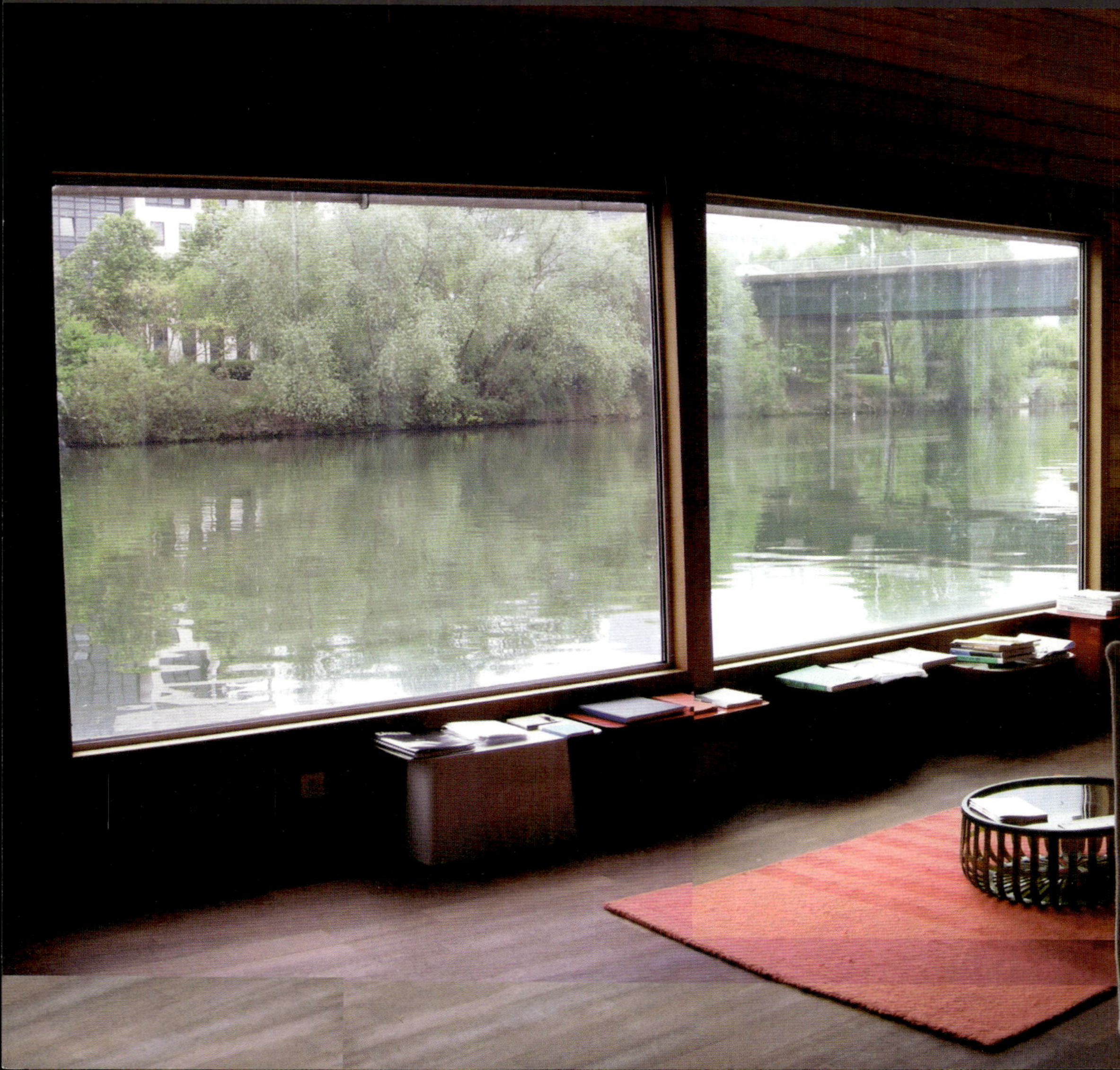

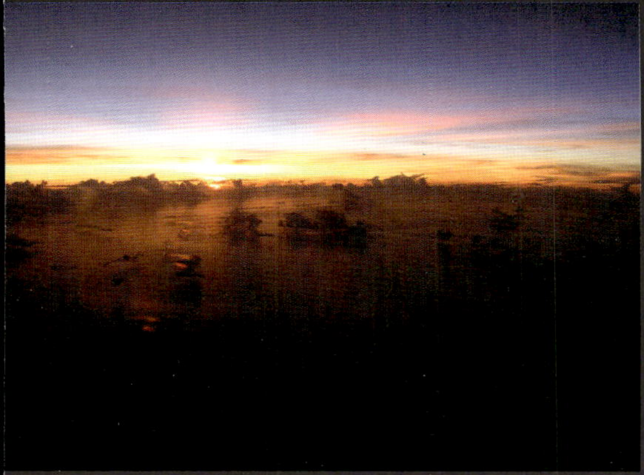

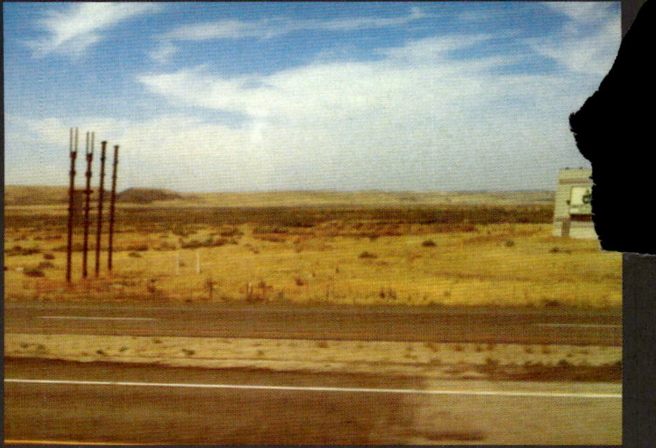

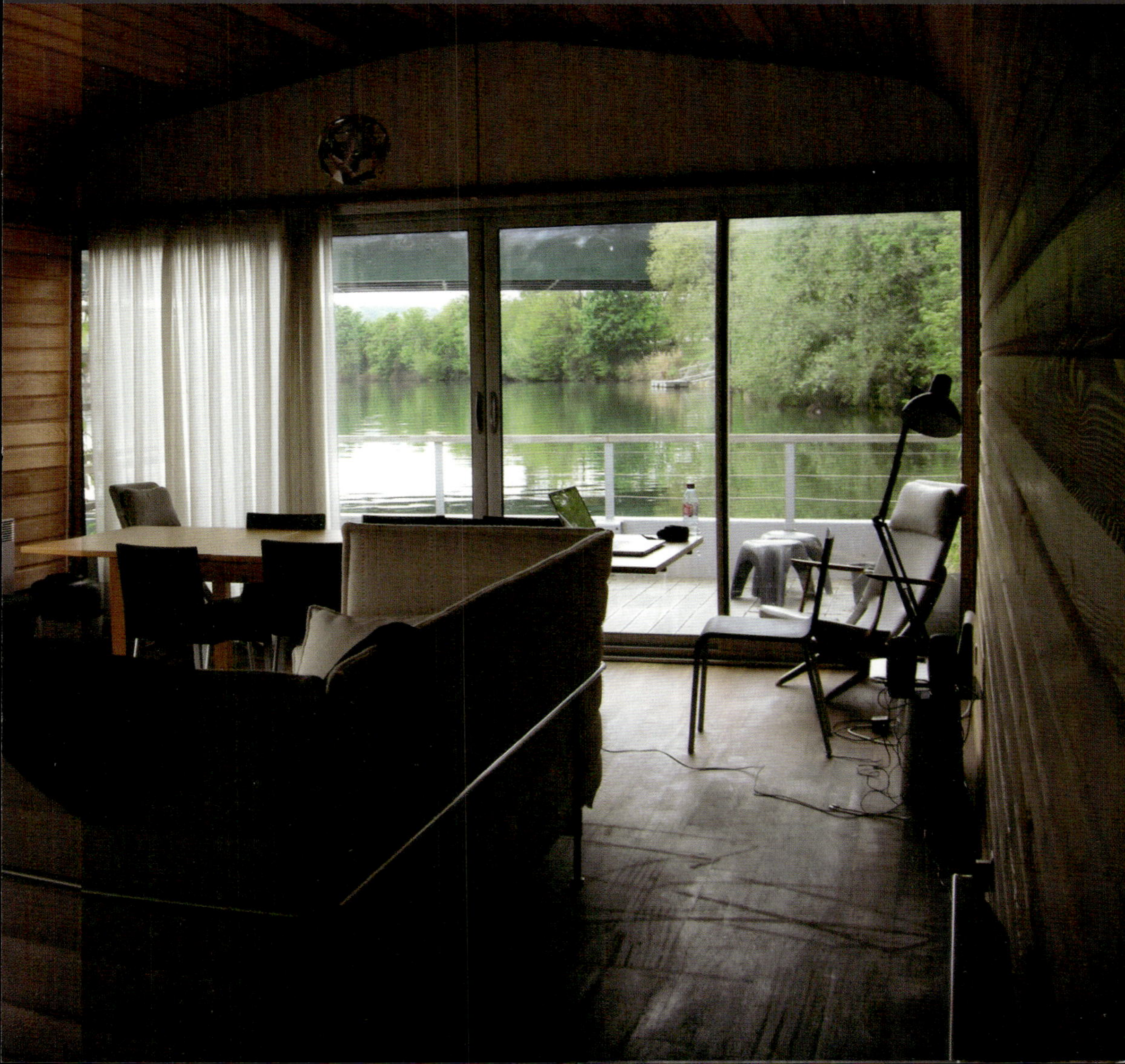

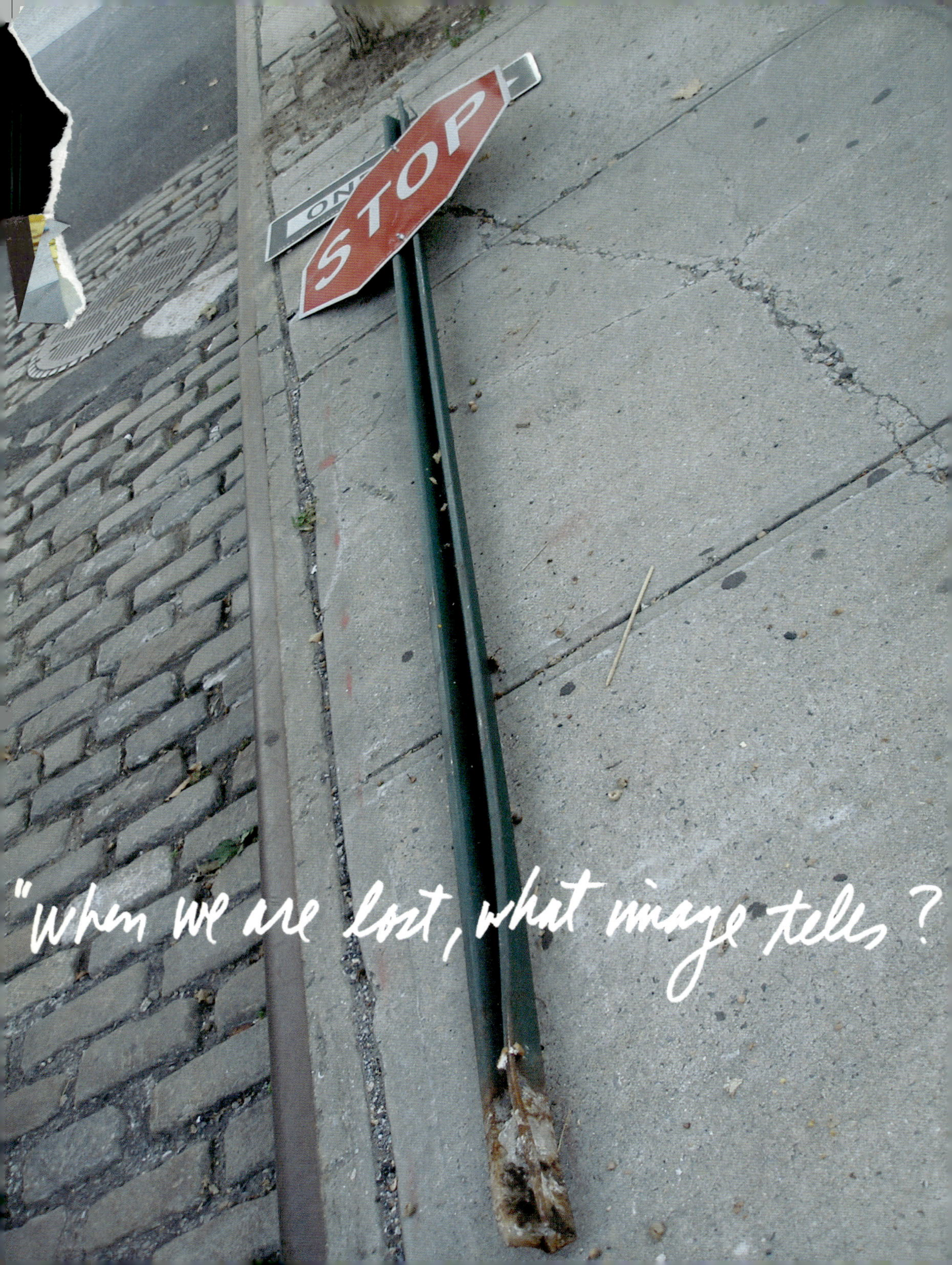
STOP
"when we are lost, what image tells?

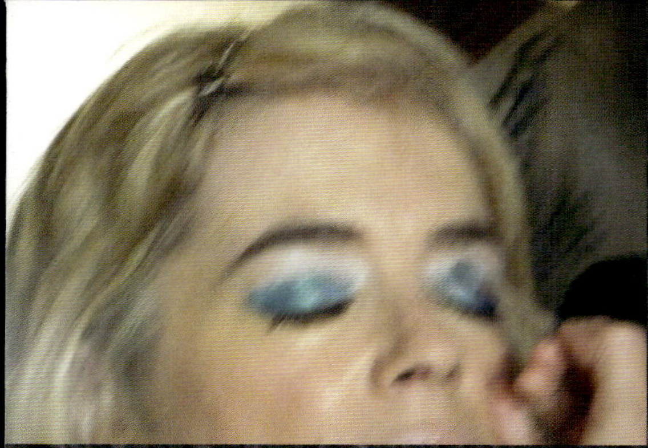
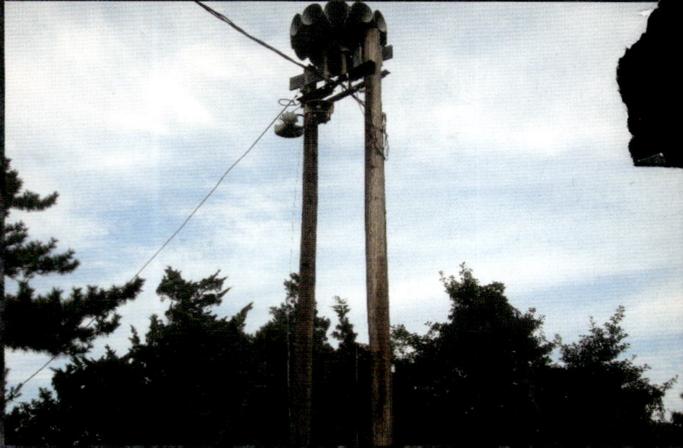
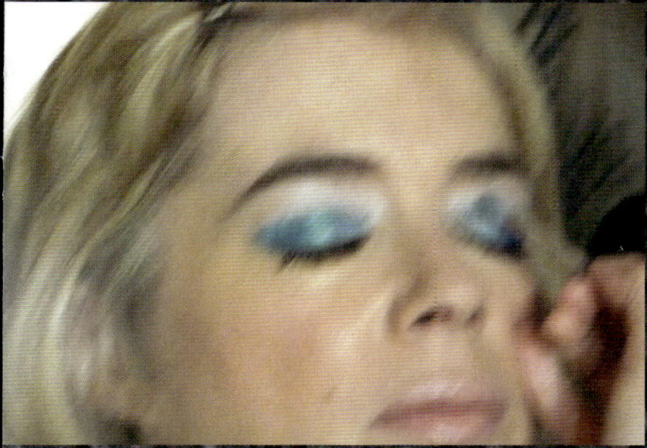
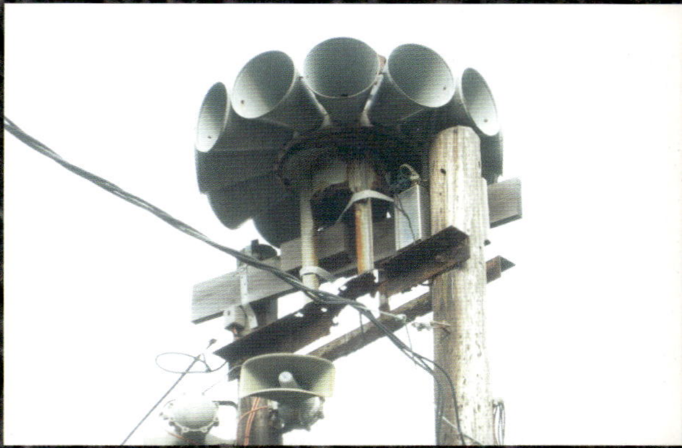
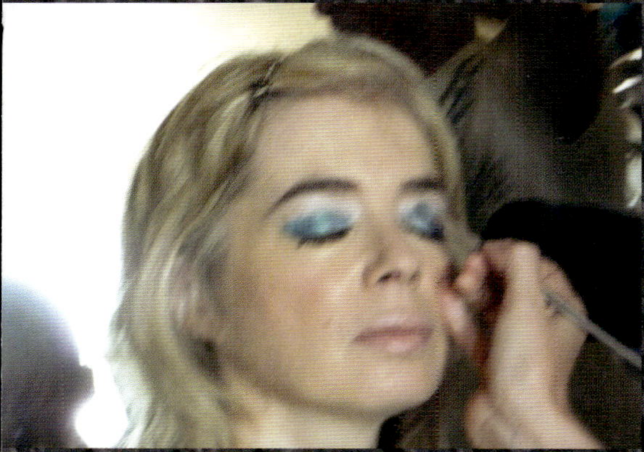
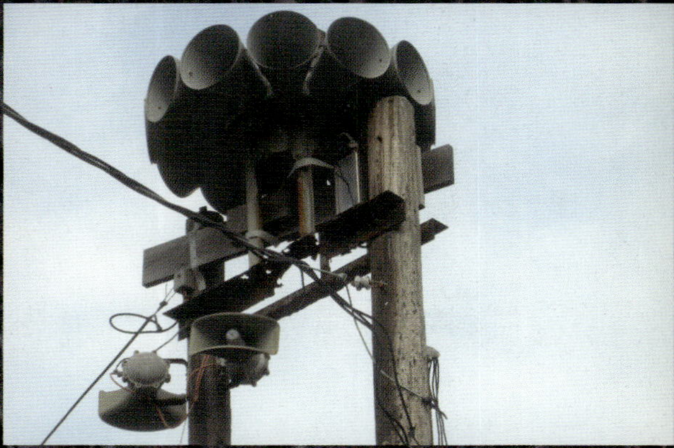

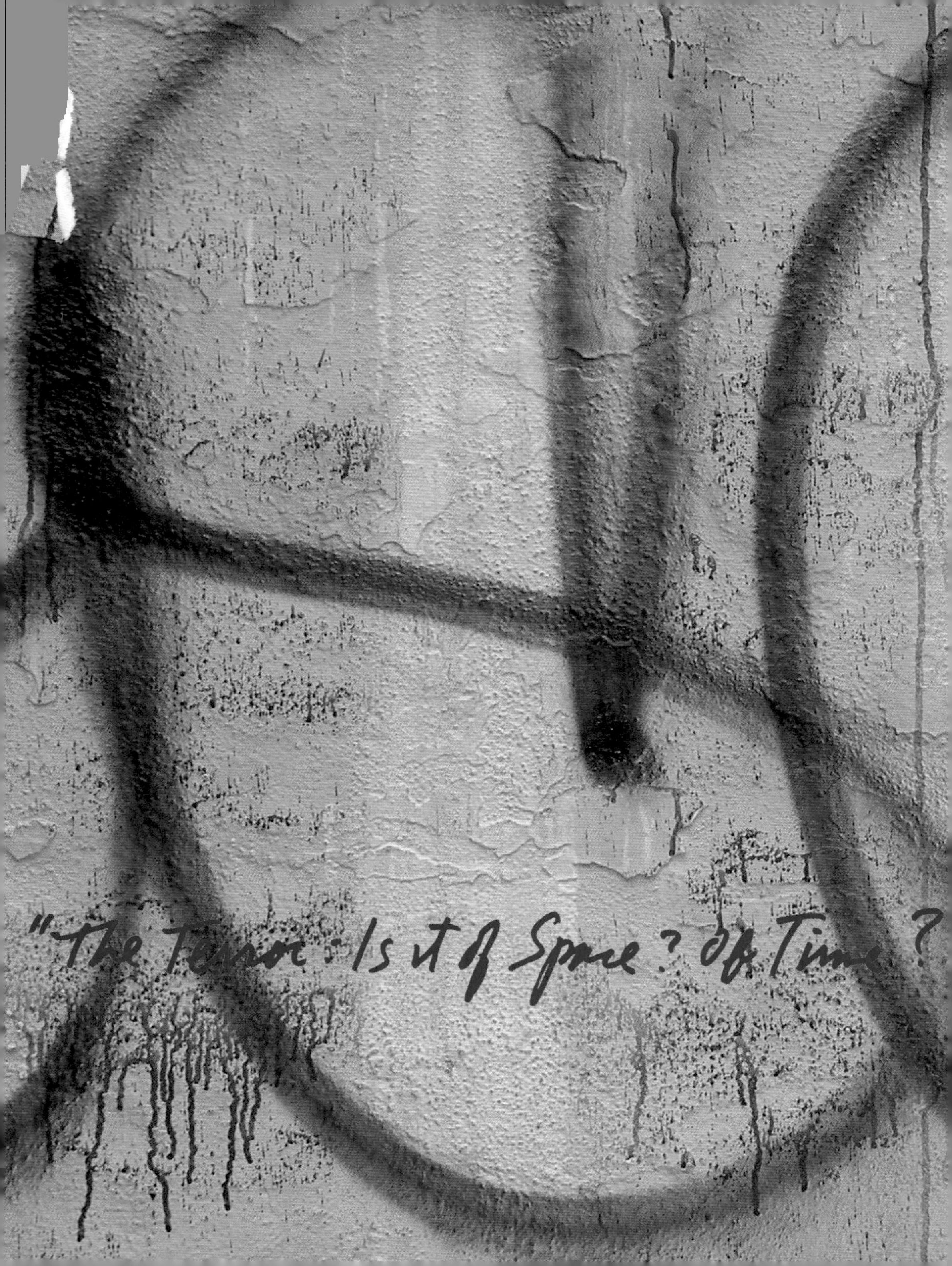
"The Terror : Is it of Space ? Of Time ?

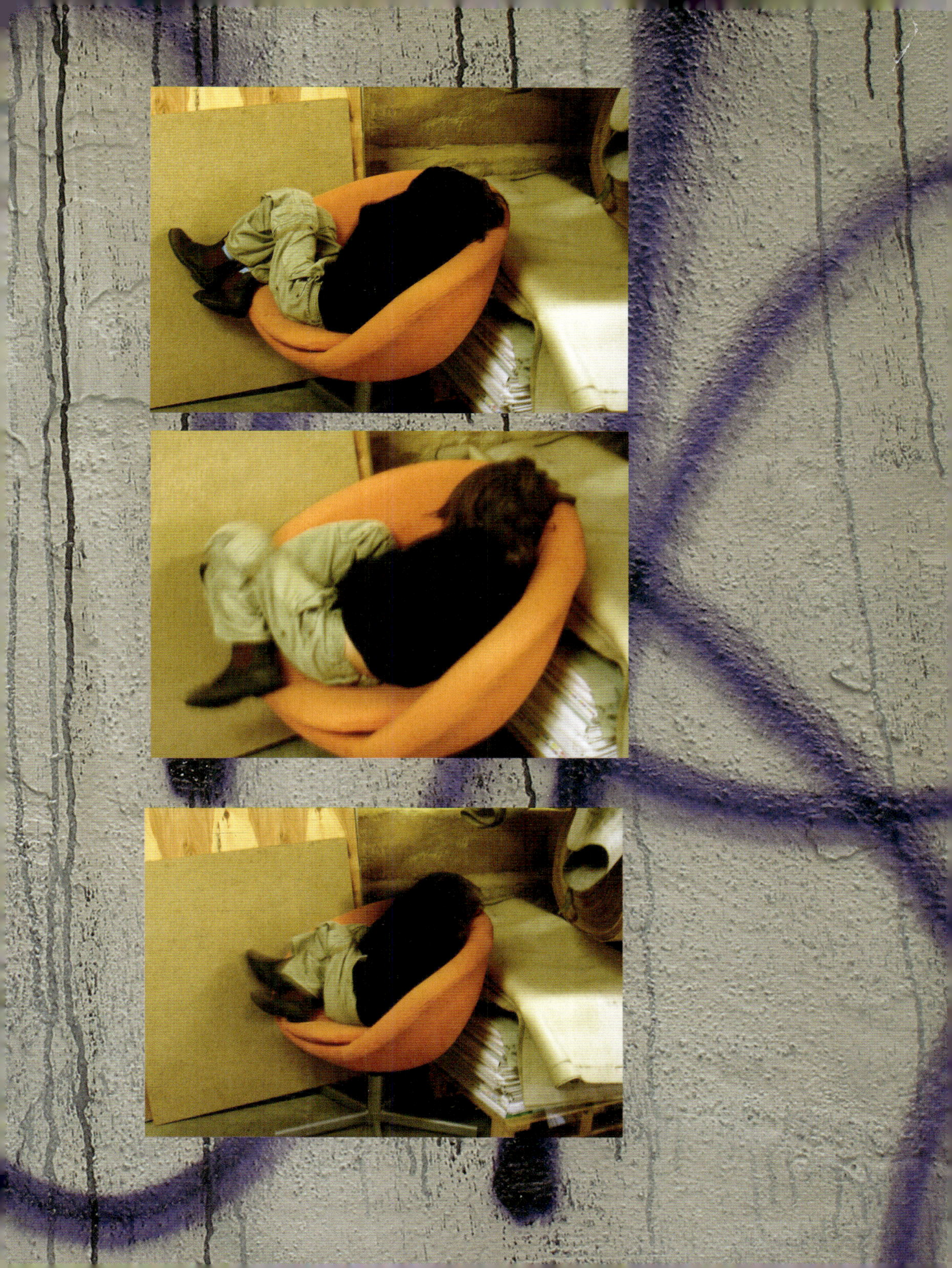

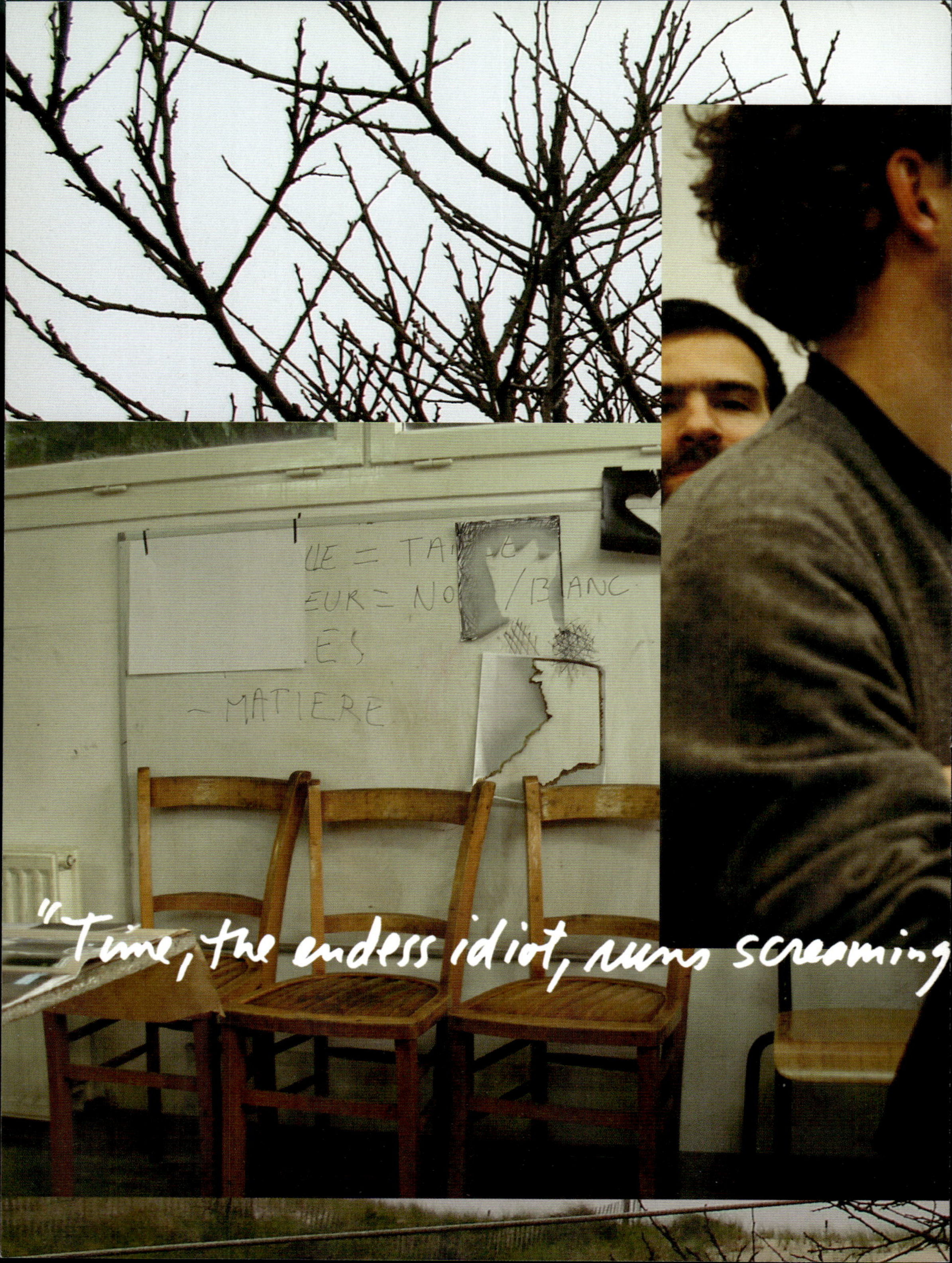
"Time, the endess idiot, runs screaming
MATIERE

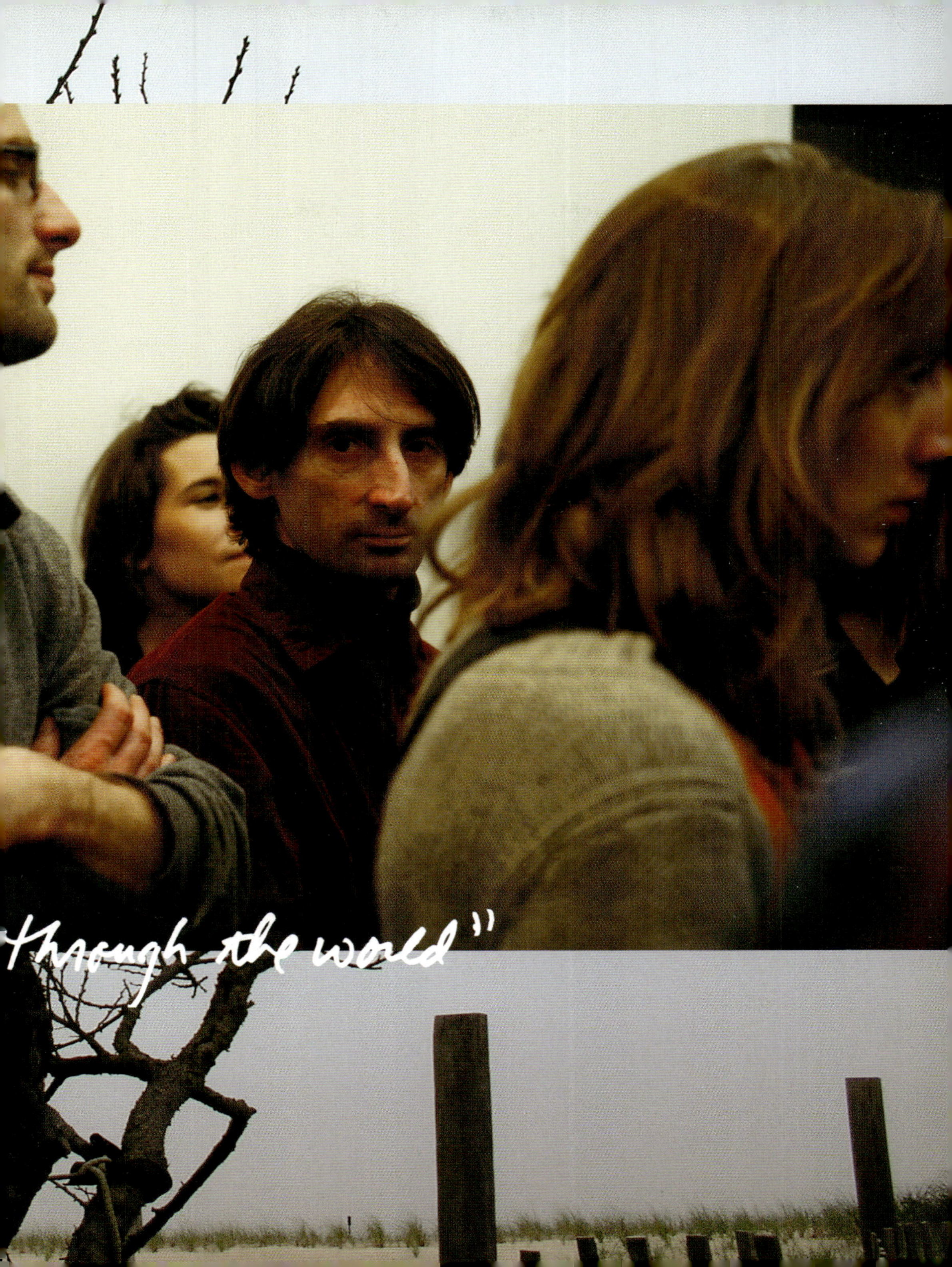
through the world"

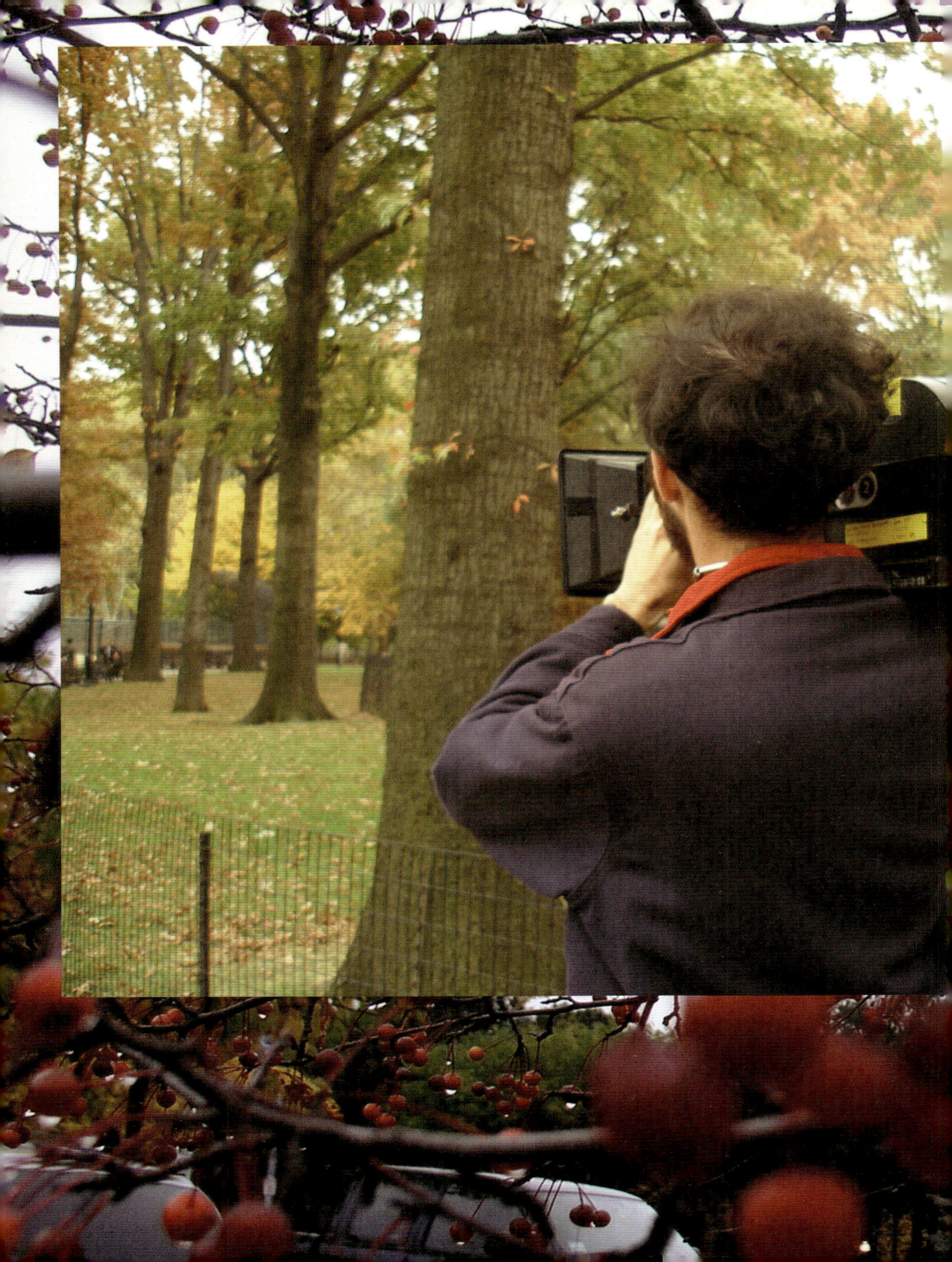

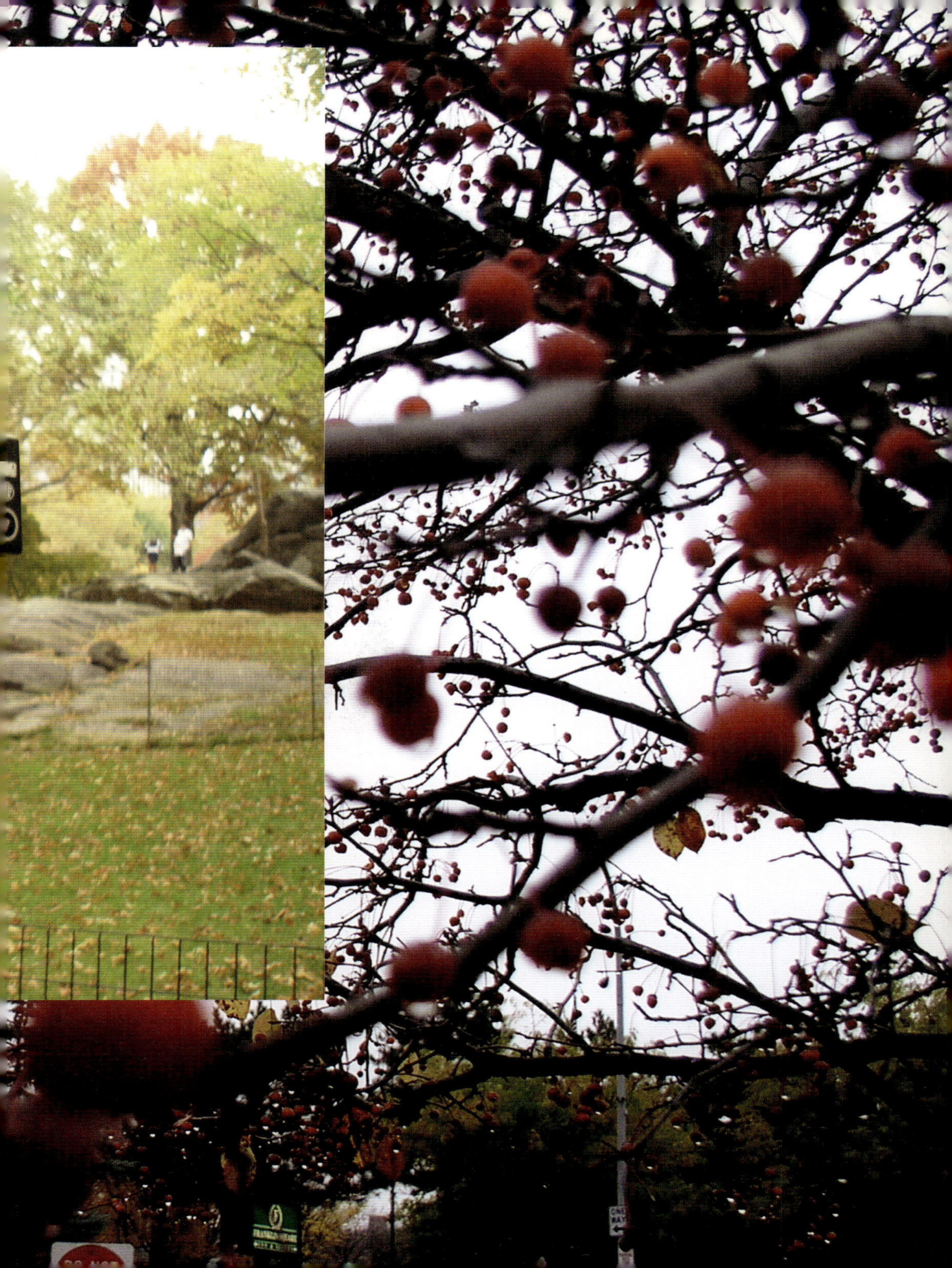

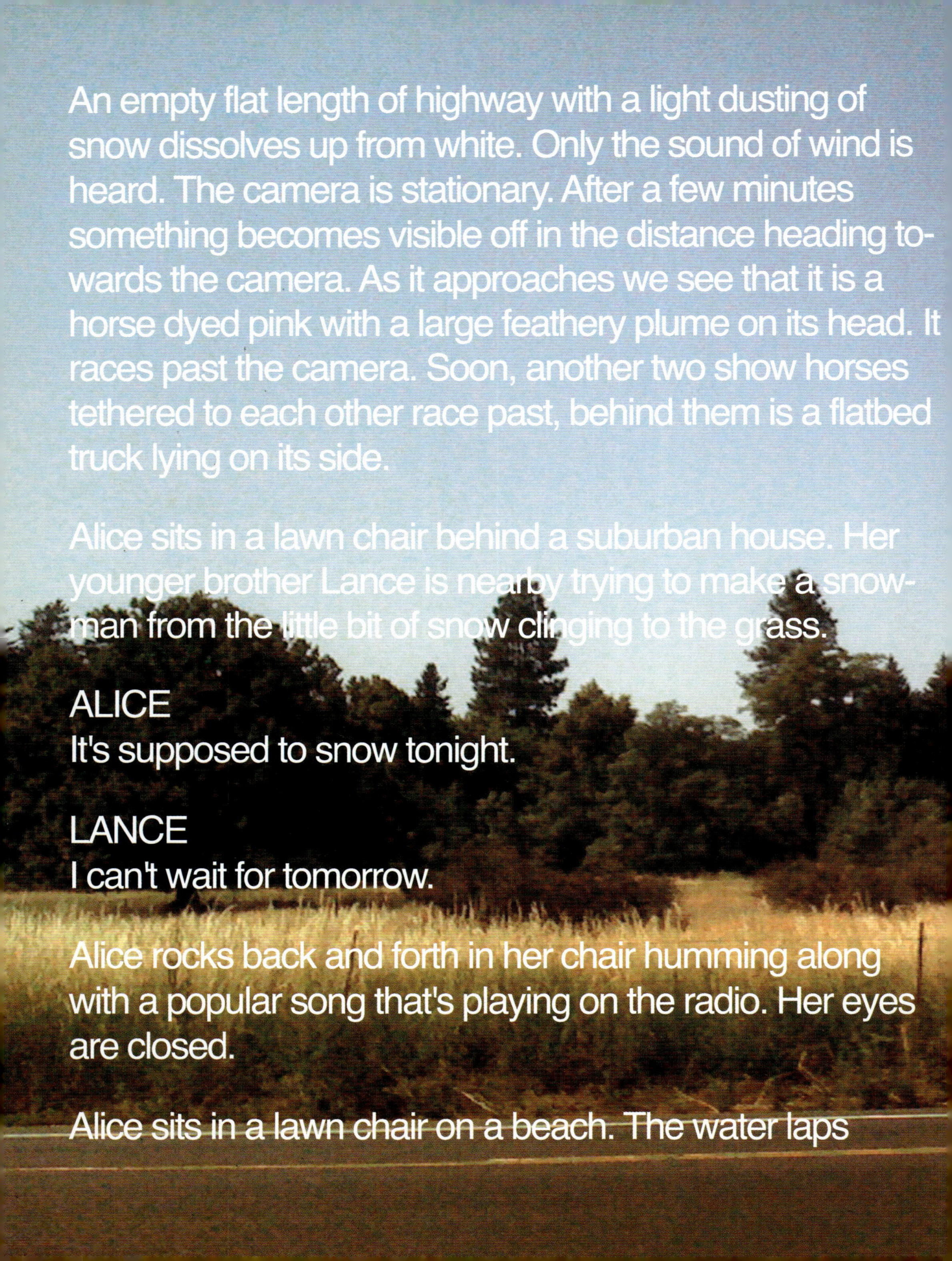

An empty flat length of highway with a light dusting of snow dissolves up from white. Only the sound of wind is heard. The camera is stationary. After a few minutes something becomes visible off in the distance heading towards the camera. As it approaches we see that it is a horse dyed pink with a large feathery plume on its head. It races past the camera. Soon, another two show horses tethered to each other race past, behind them is a flatbed truck lying on its side.

Alice sits in a lawn chair behind a suburban house. Her younger brother Lance is nearby trying to make a snowman from the little bit of snow clinging to the grass.

ALICE
It's supposed to snow tonight.

LANCE
I can't wait for tomorrow.

Alice rocks back and forth in her chair humming along with a popular song that's playing on the radio. Her eyes are closed.

Alice sits in a lawn chair on a beach. The water laps

around her feet. She wears a big fashionable straw hat and severe sunglasses. Her brother is building a tiered sandcastle nearby. The same radio song is playing.

LANCE
Where've ya been?

ALICE
Nowhere.

LANCE
Your eyes were closed and you were kinda mumbling something.

ALICE
I was just thinking.

LANCE
About what?

ALICE
About places I wanna go.

LANCE
What do you mean? Where are you going?

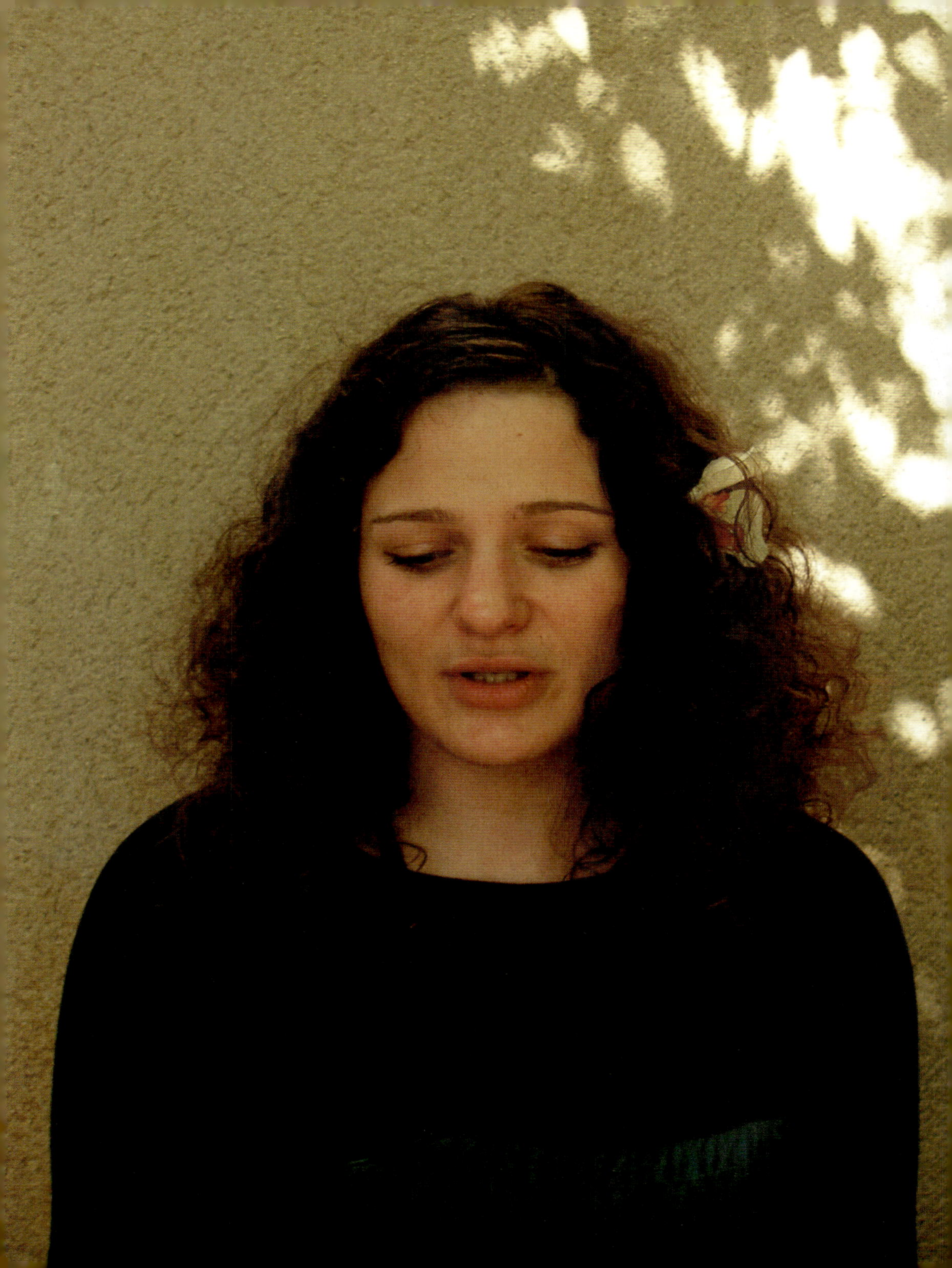

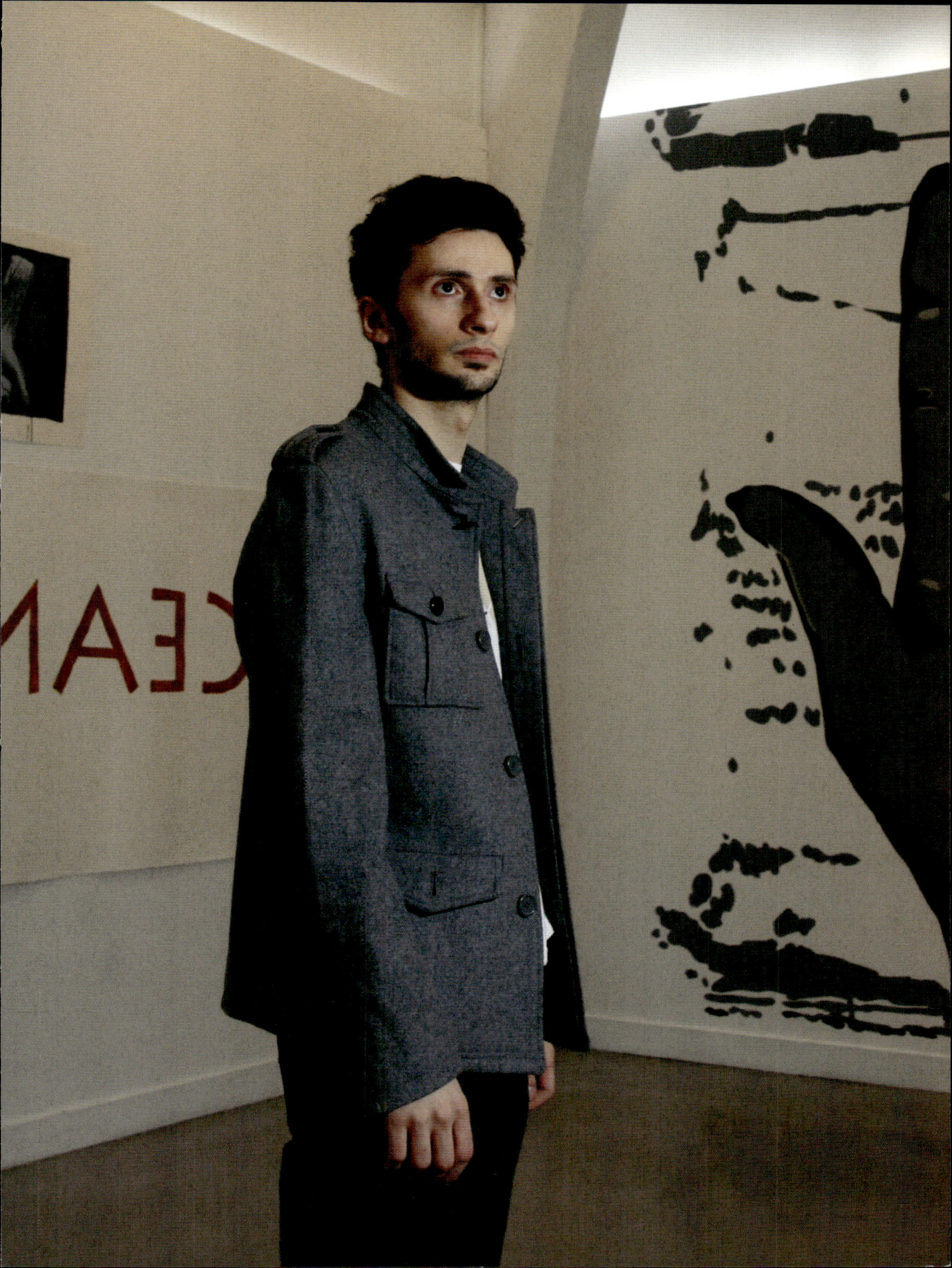

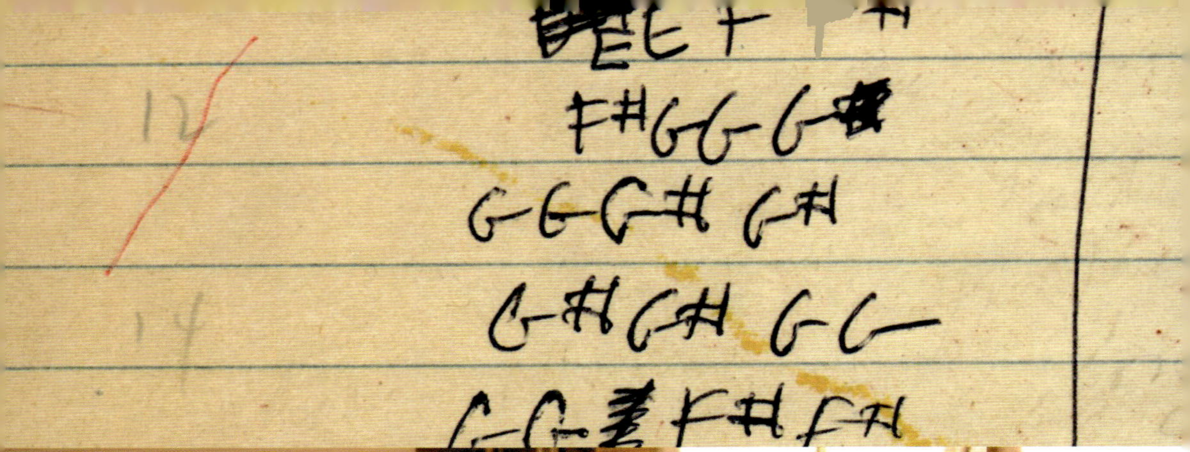
F#GGG#
GGG#G#
G#G#GG

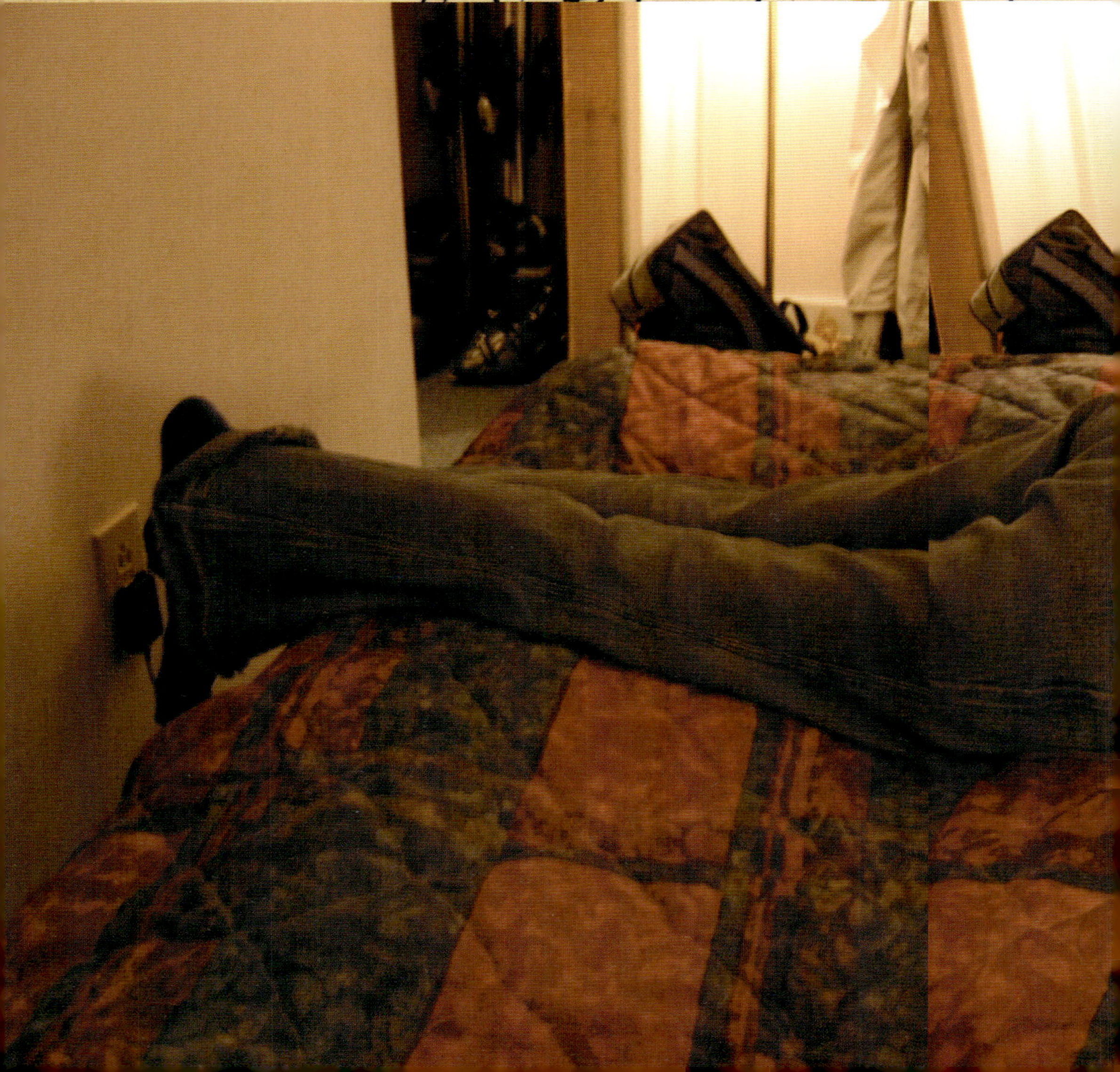

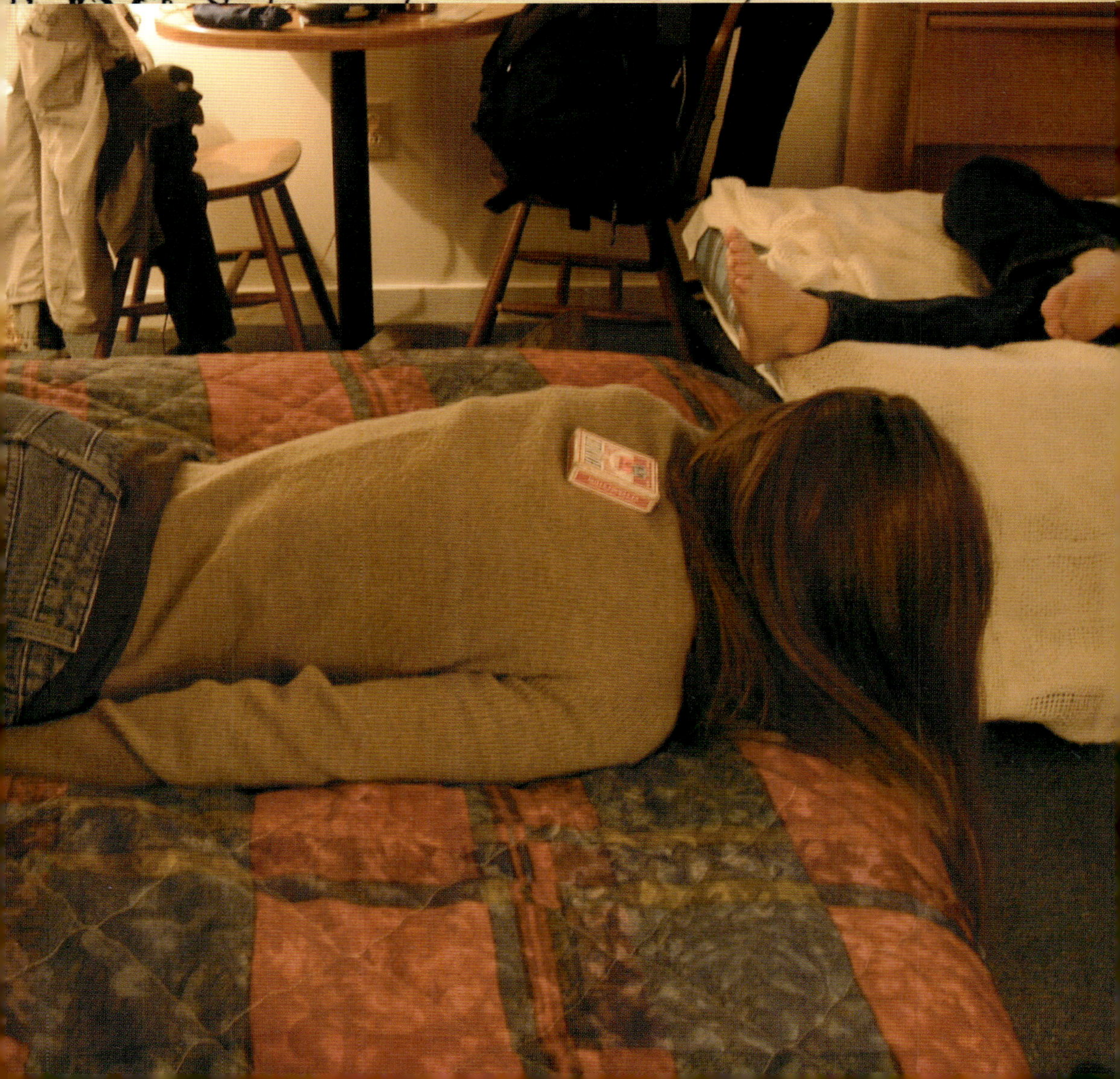

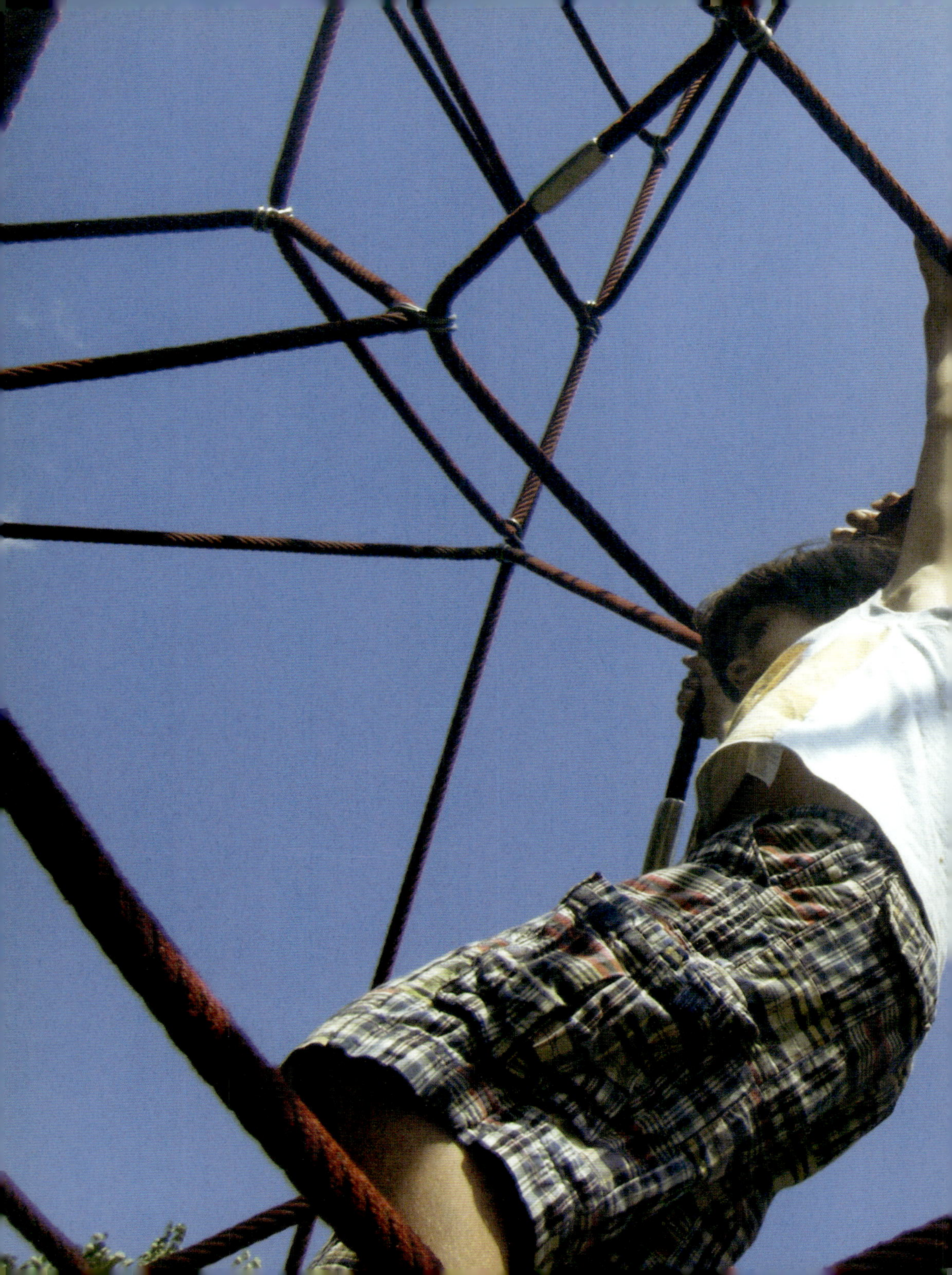

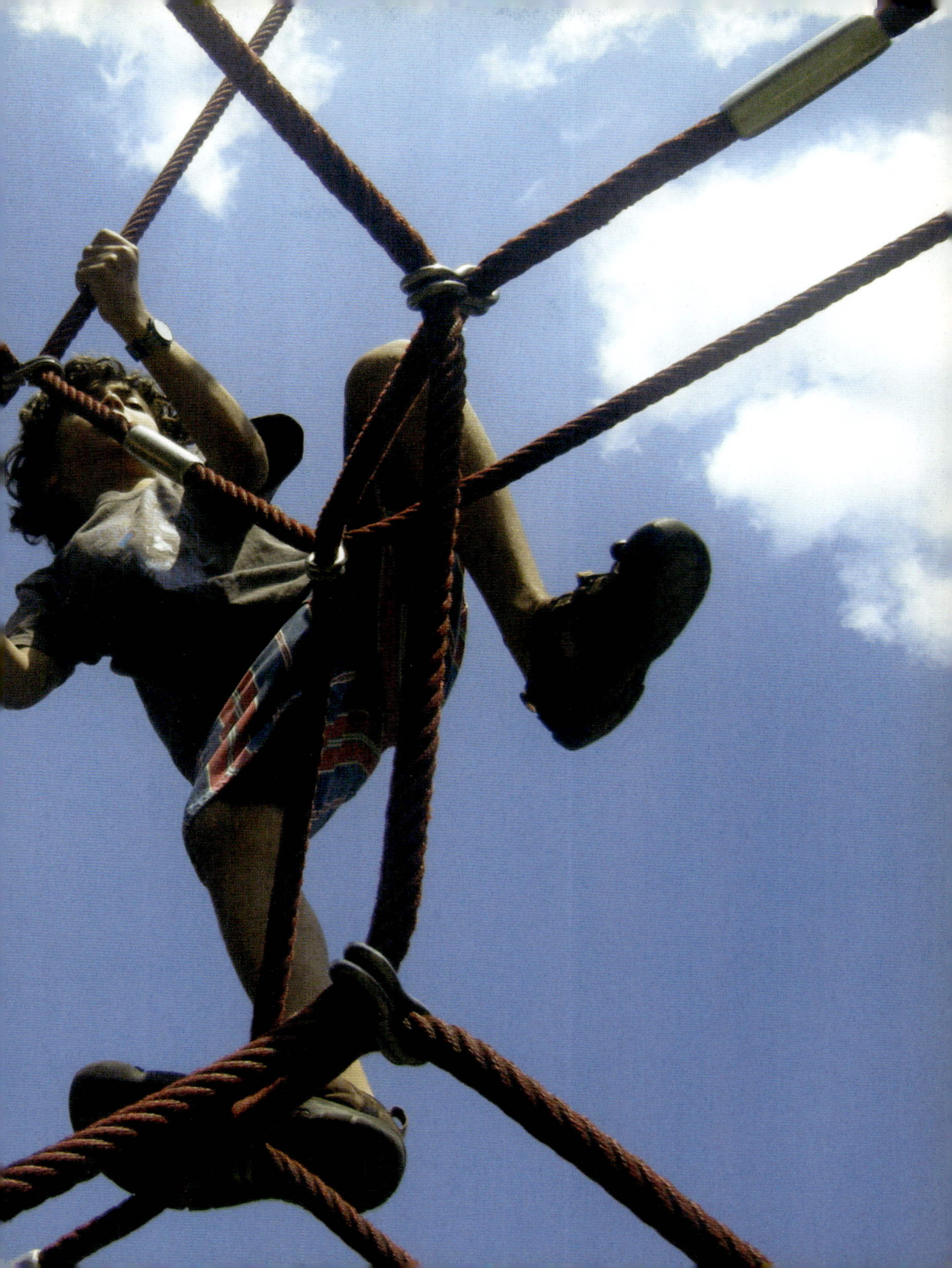

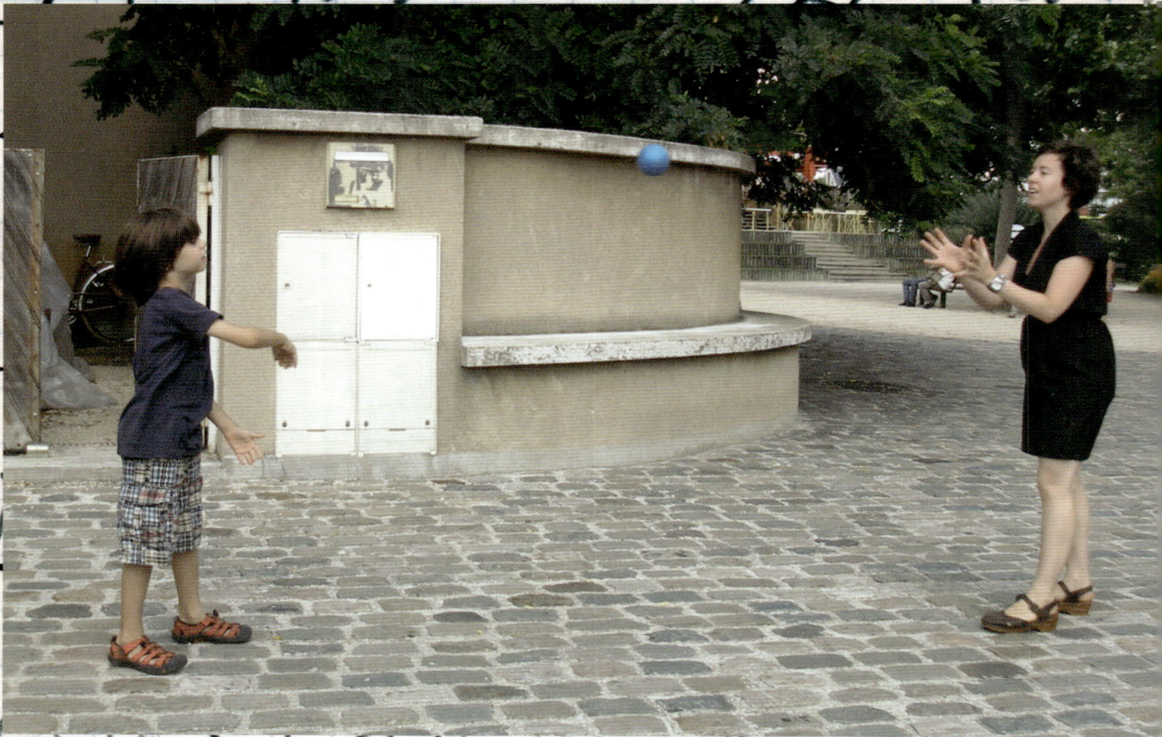

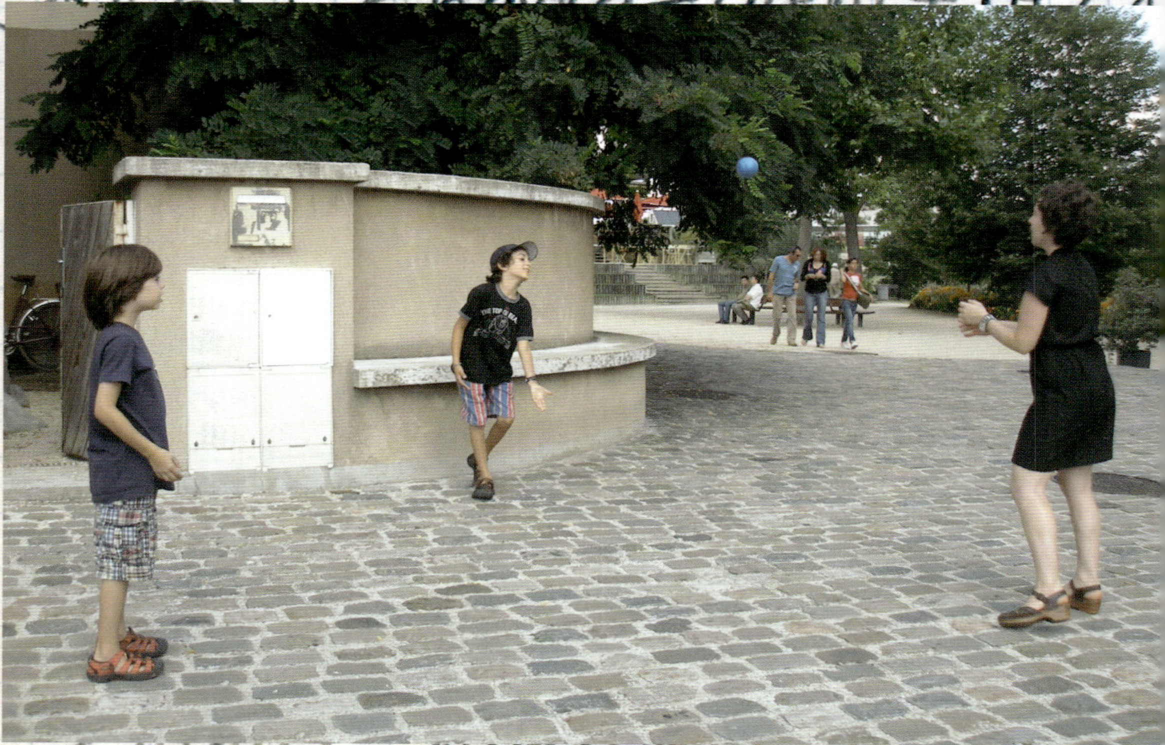

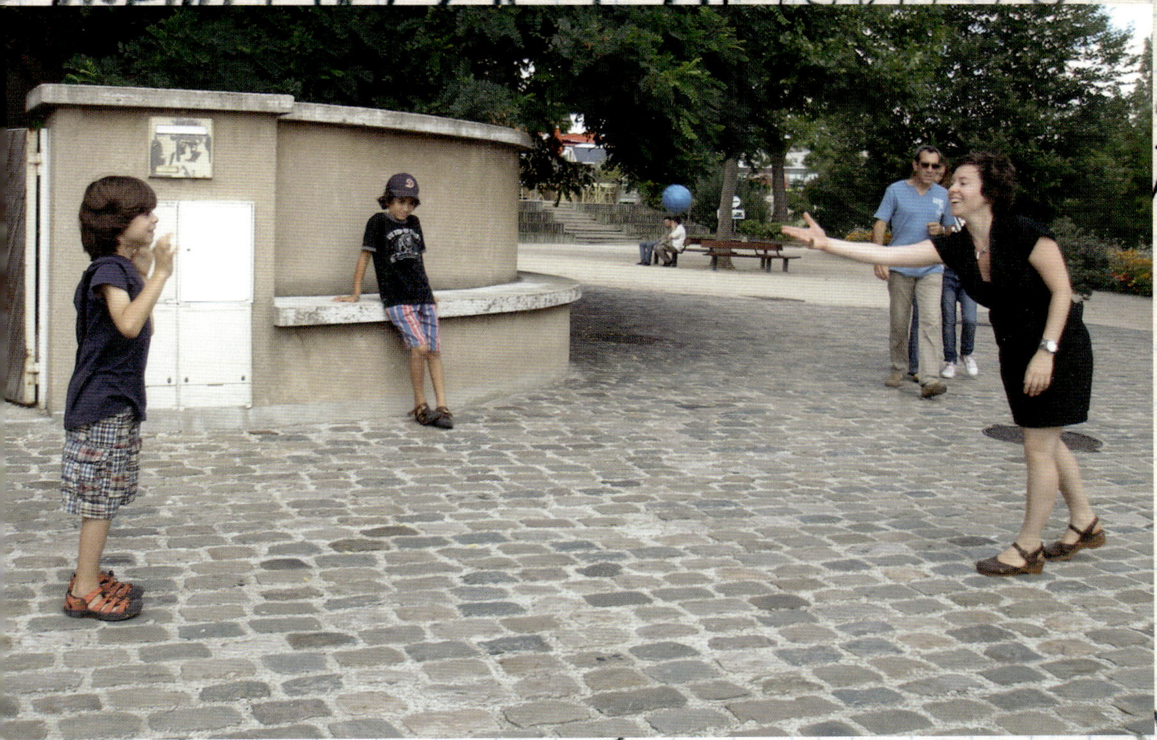

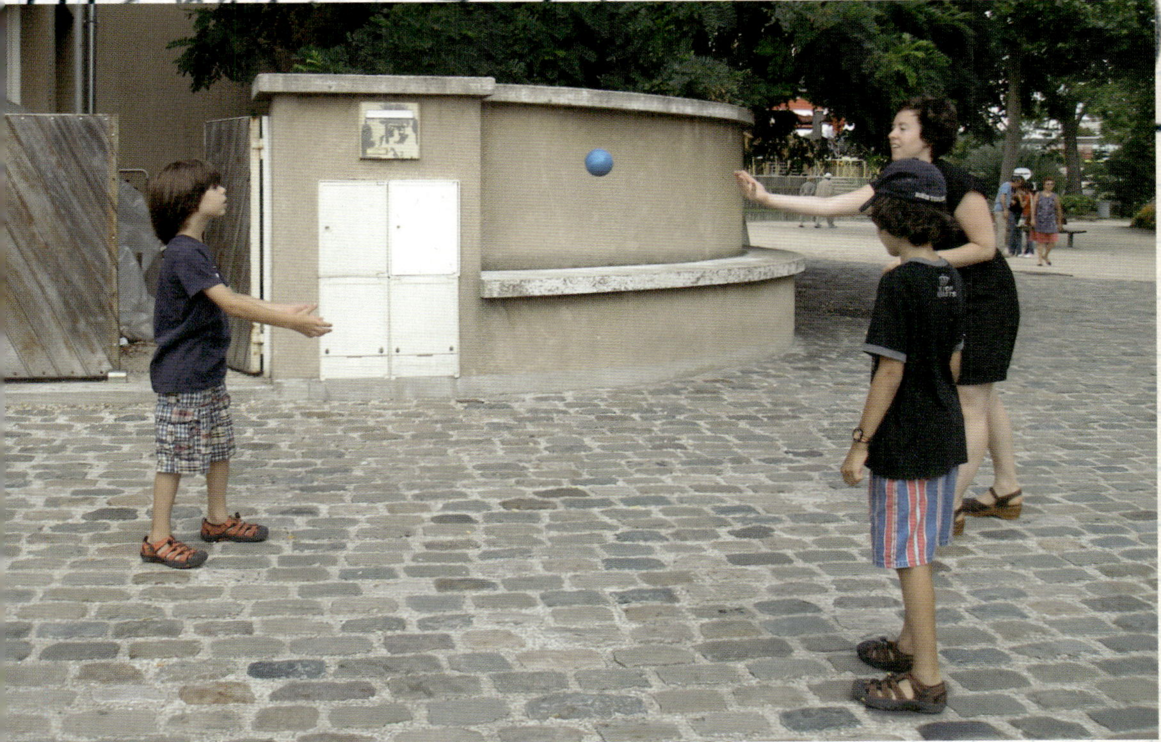

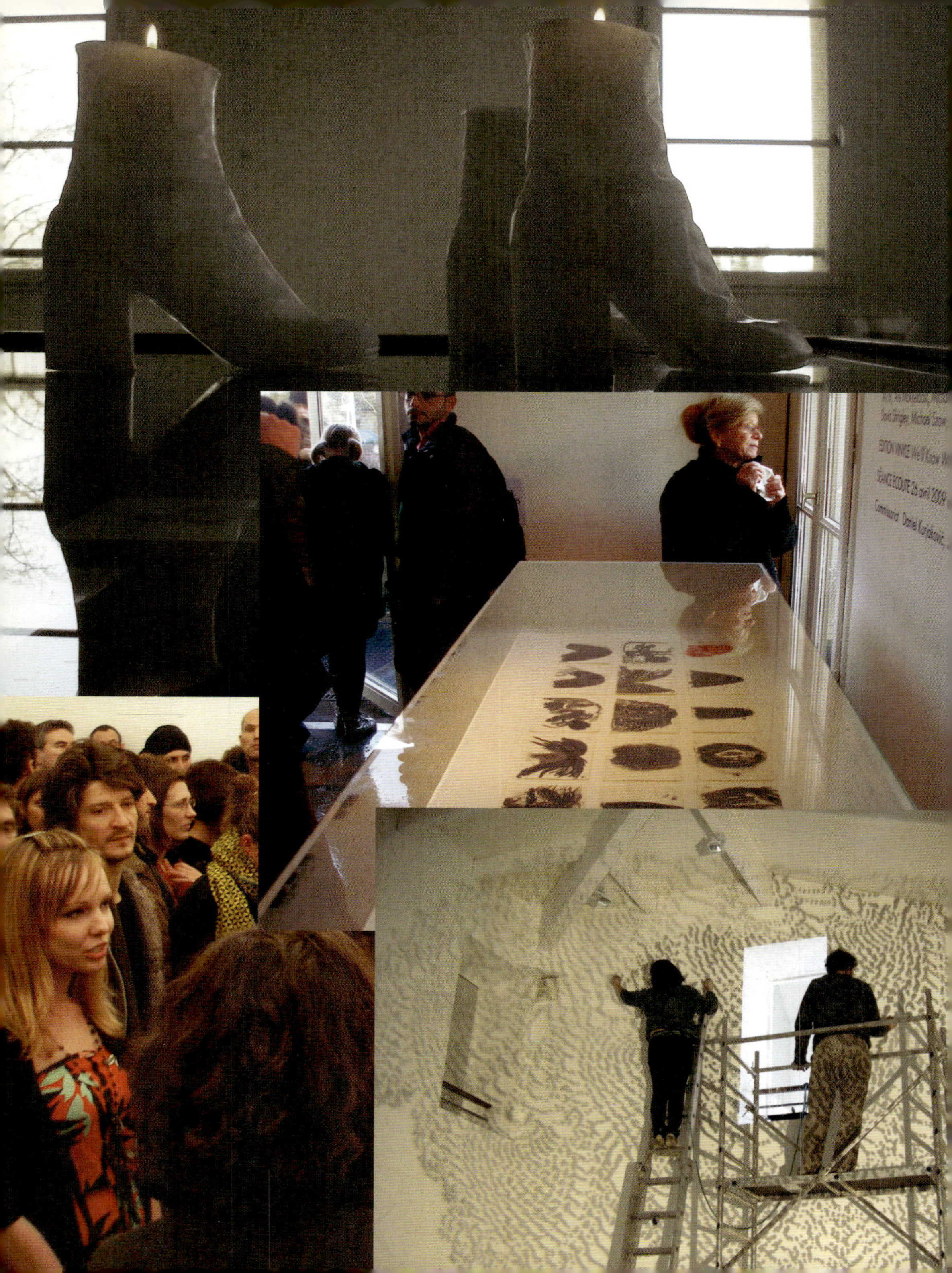

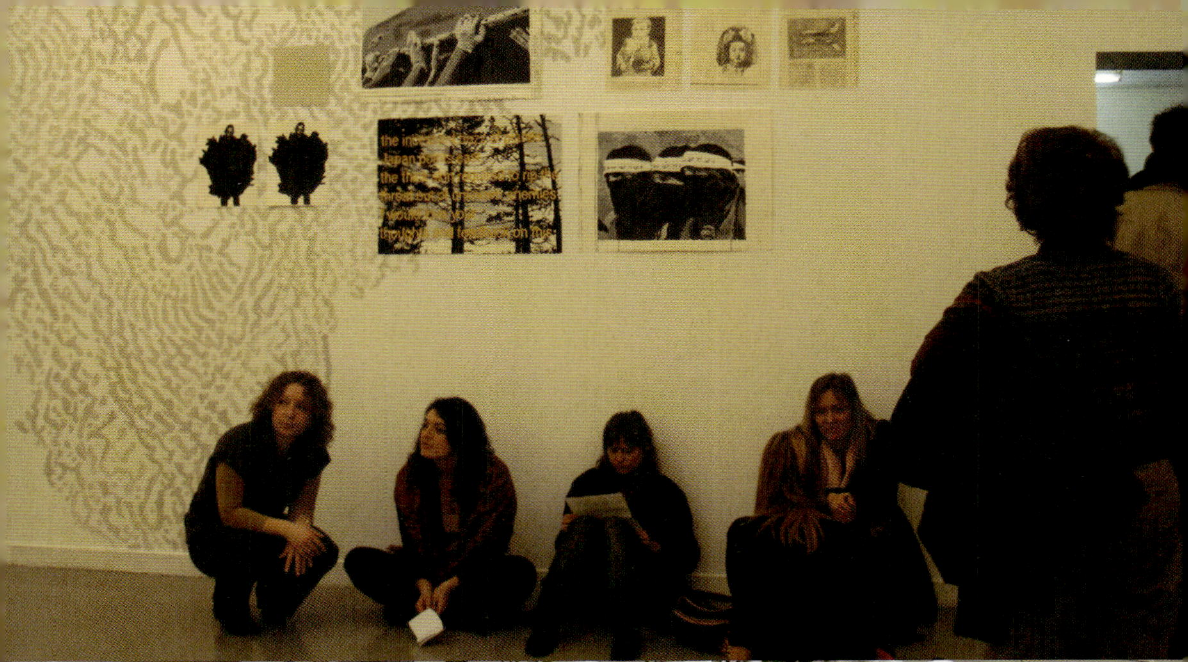

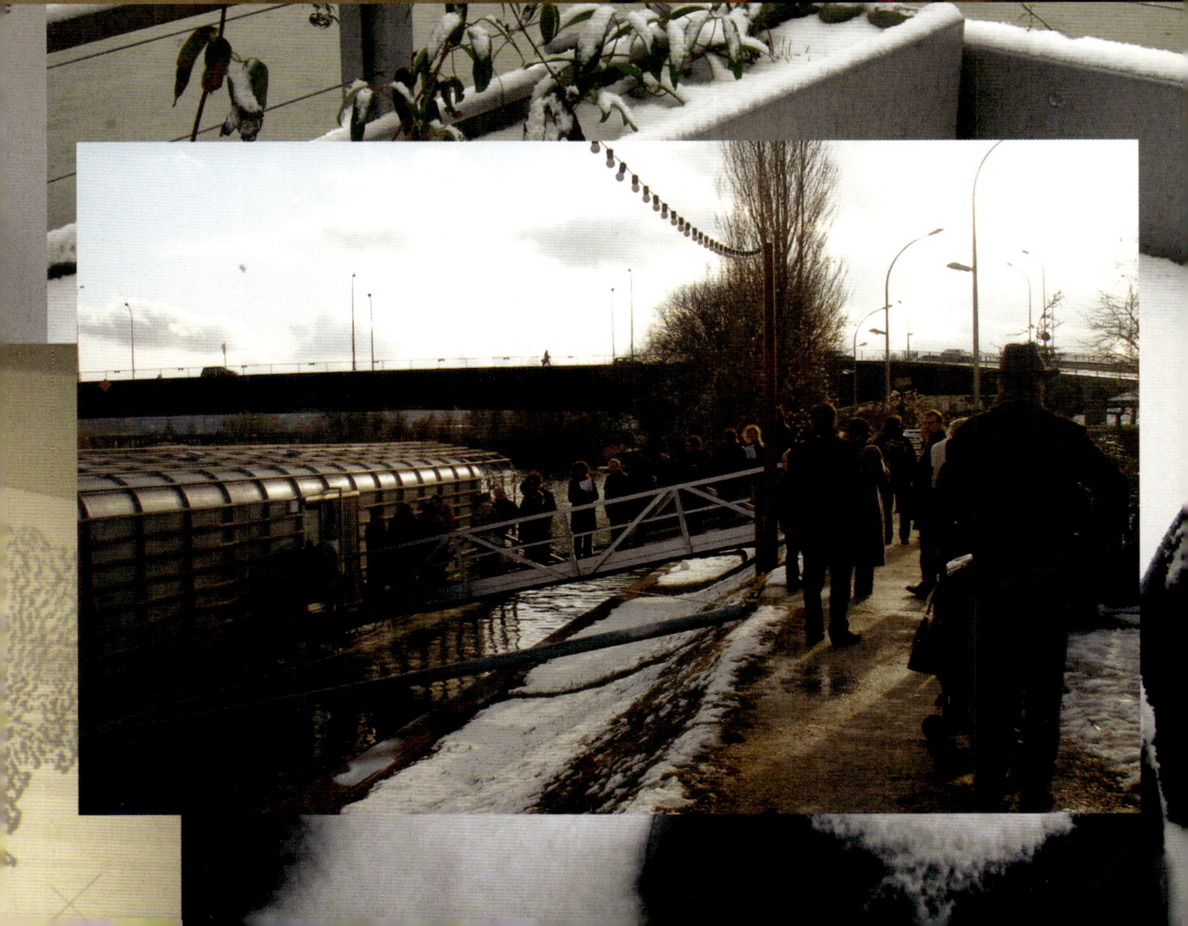

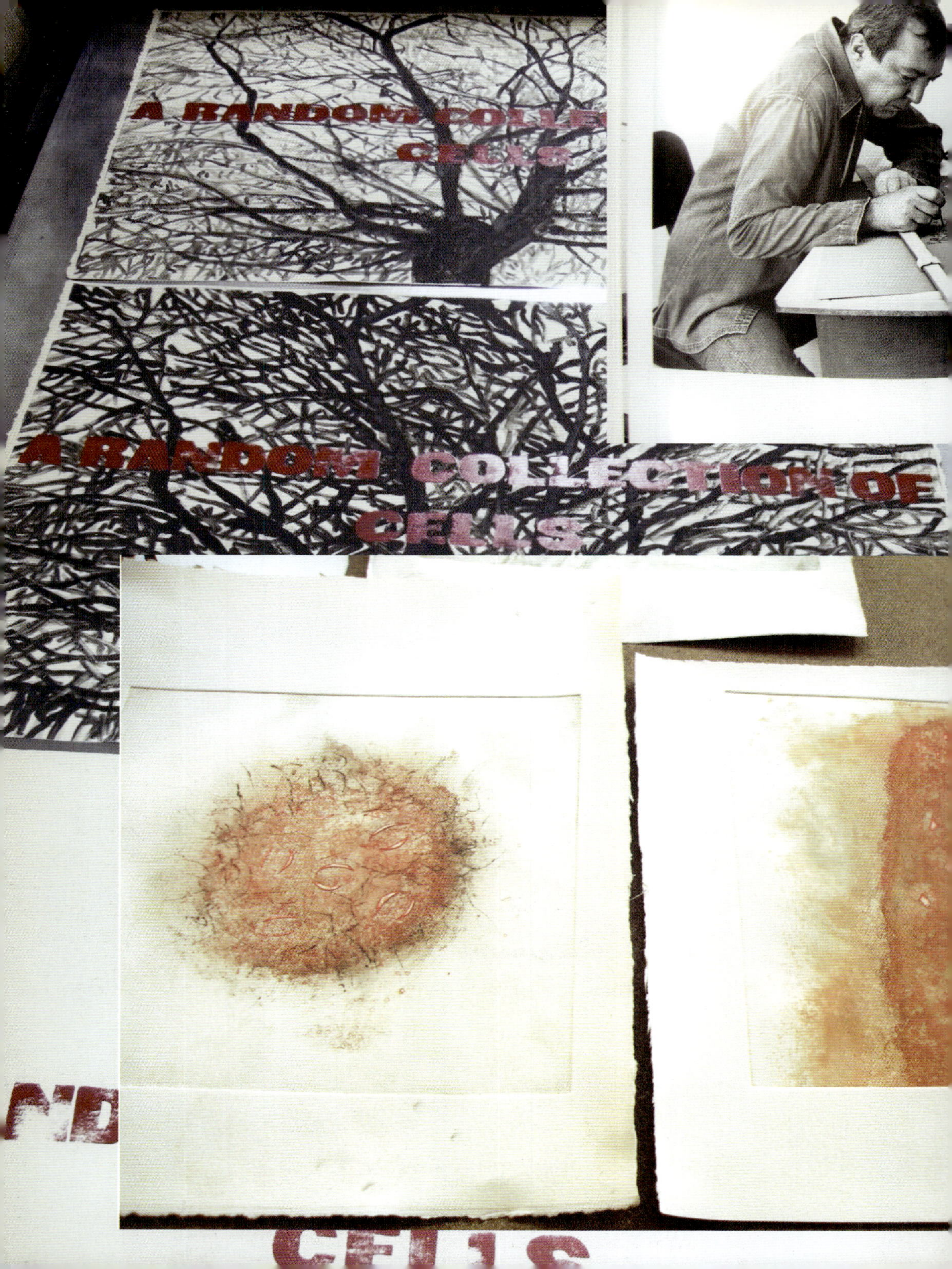
A RANDOM
CELLS
A RANDOM COLLECTION OF
CELLS

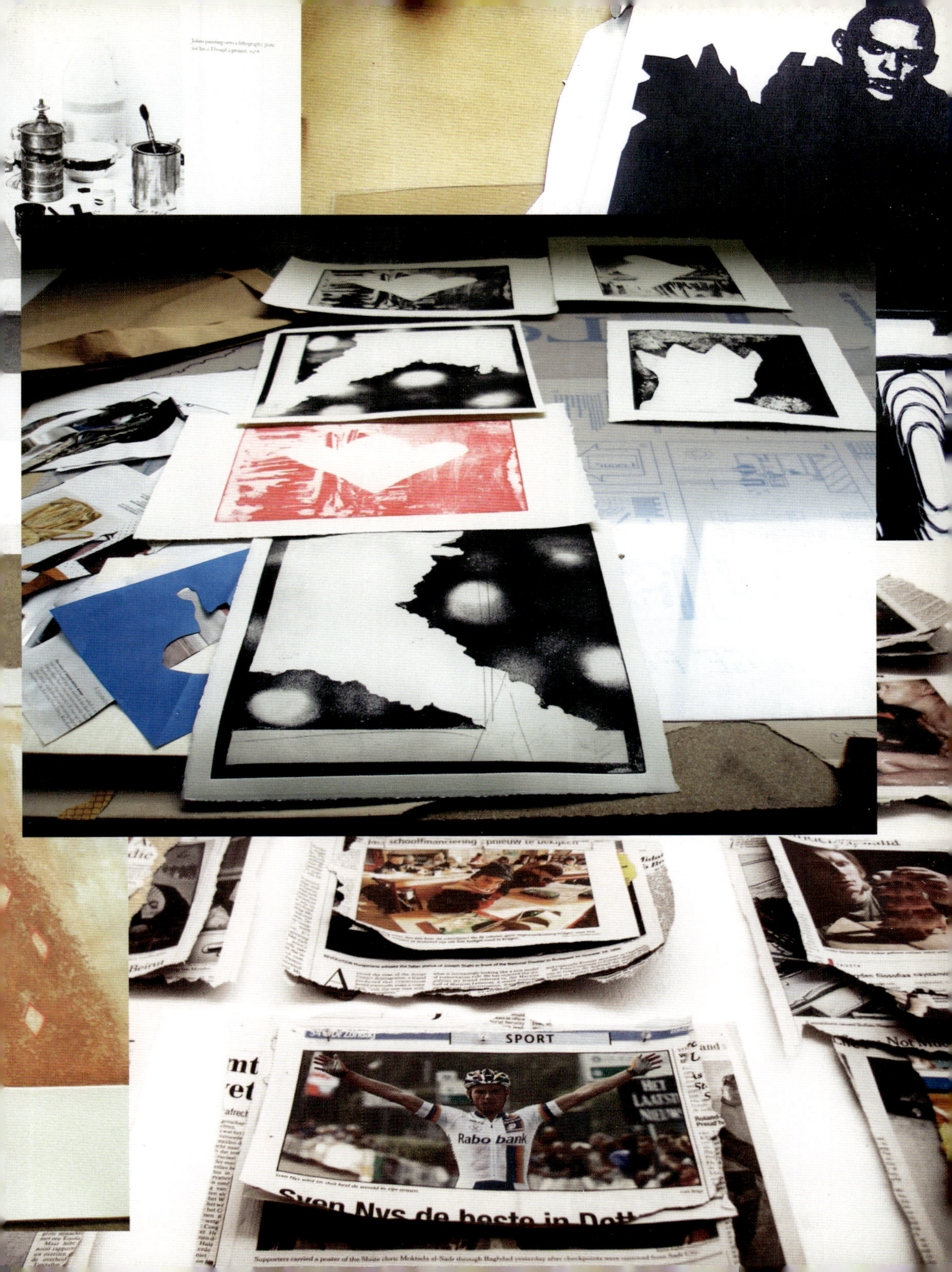
SPORT
Rabo bank
Supporters carried a poster of the Shiite cleric Moktada al-Sadr through Baghdad yesterday after checkpoints were removed from Sadr

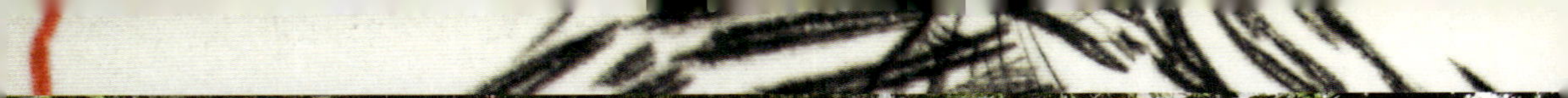
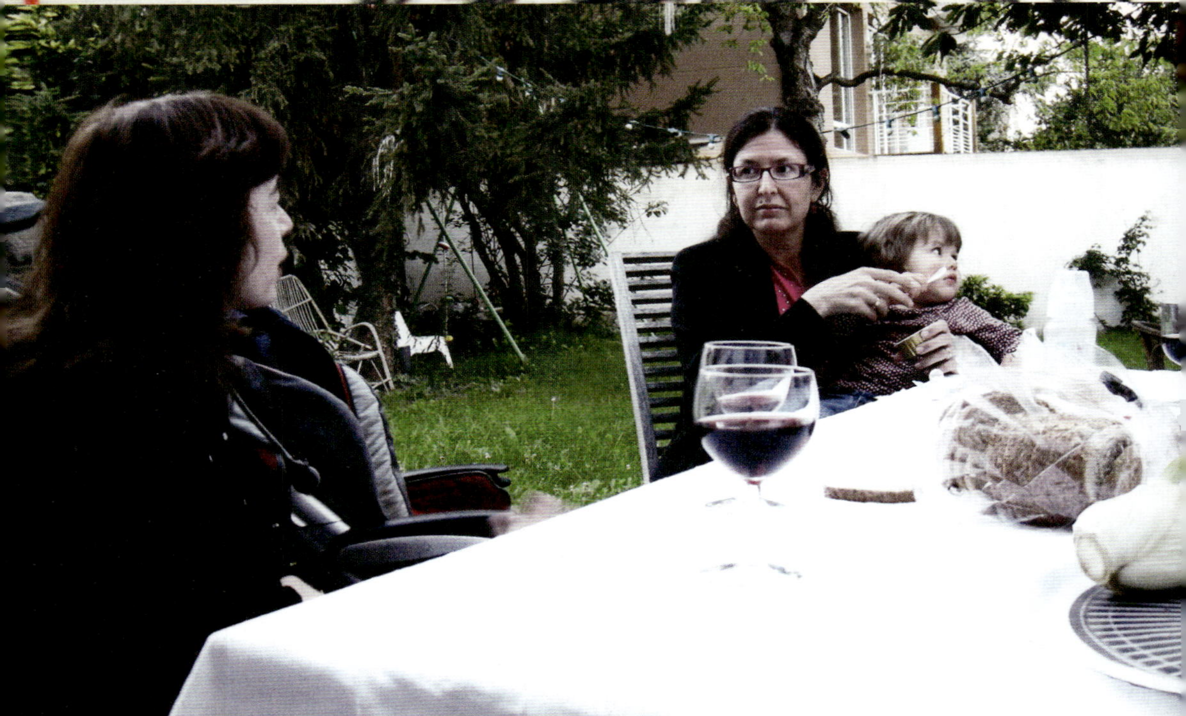
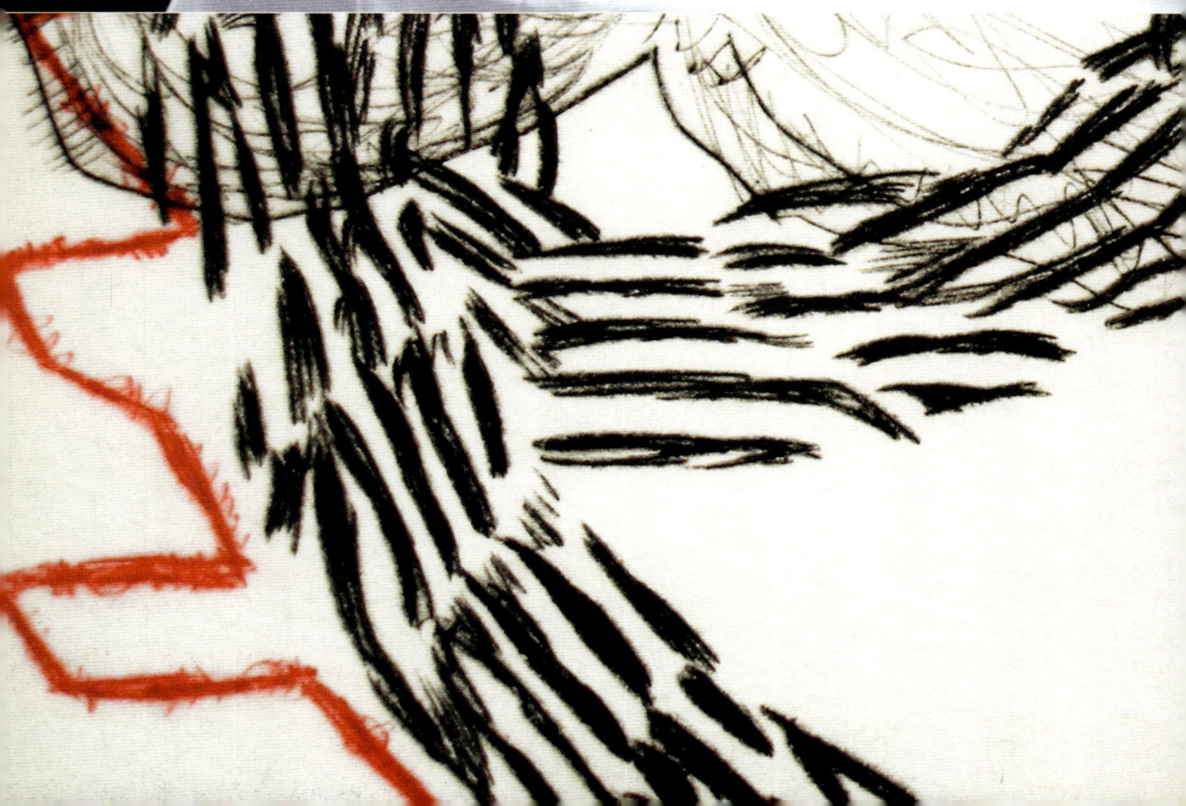

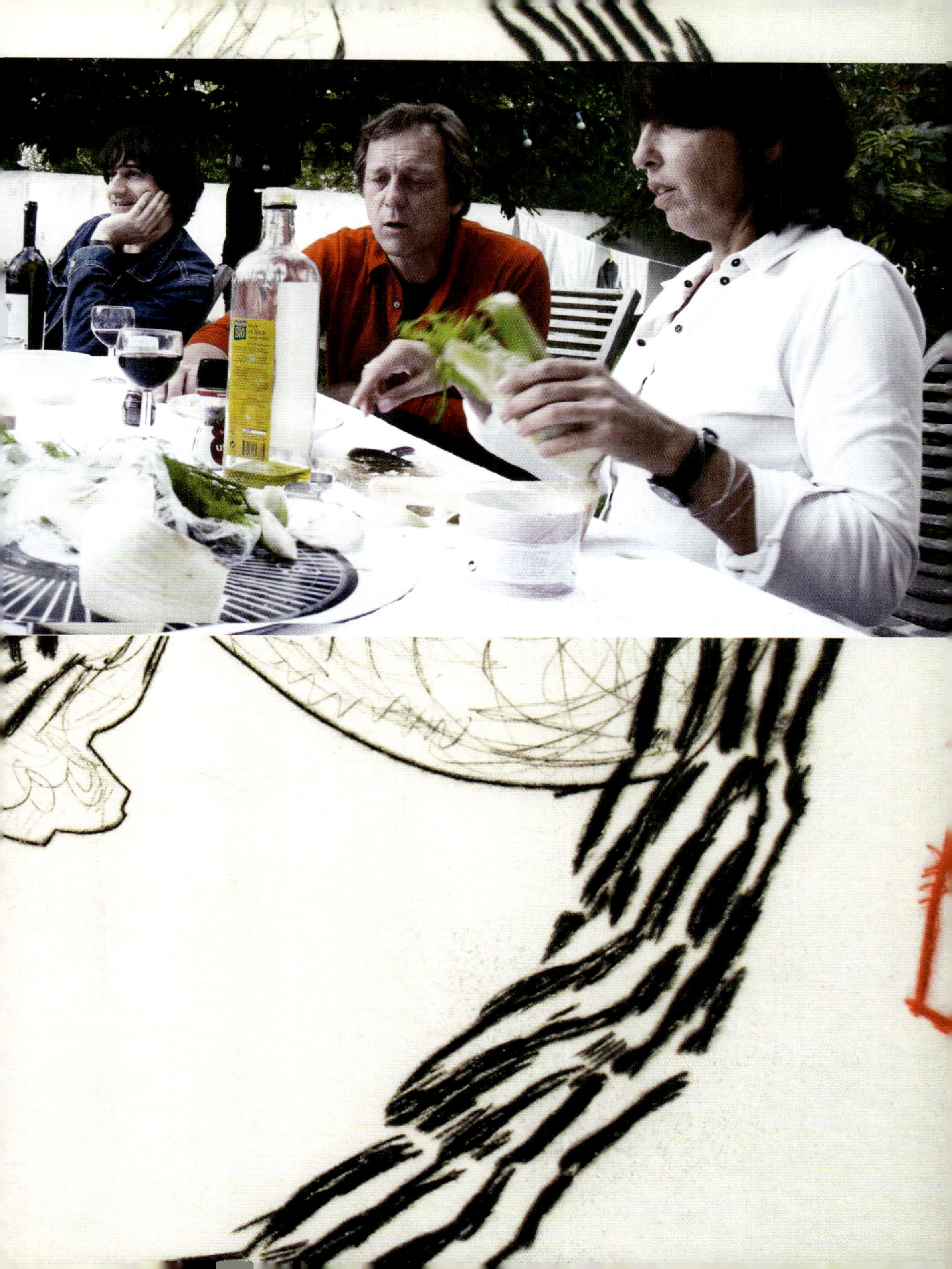

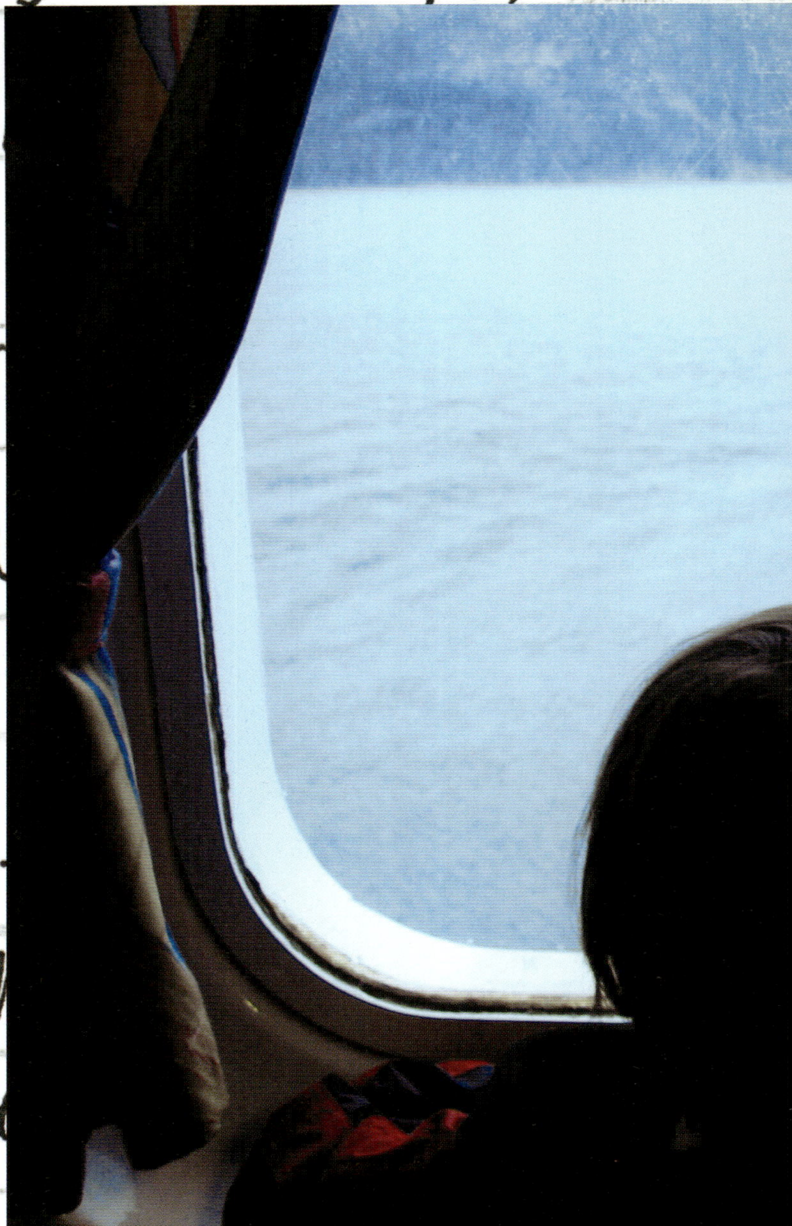

Sitting alongside the canal out the back door
the Paradiso on a slate-grey stone table
benches—the canal is glinting, bikes, cars boat
These brief trips become like little poems, ti
image-flashes. A dapper guy in small motorbo

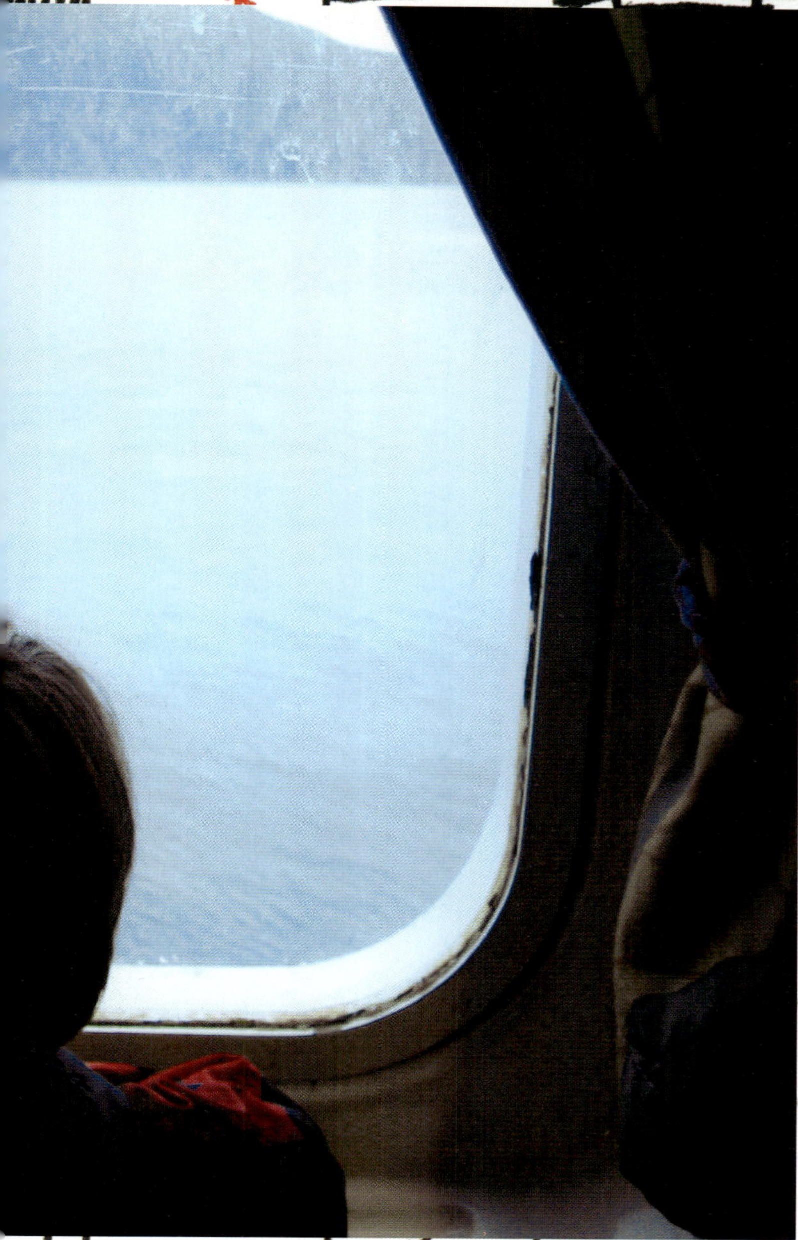

ıst drives by, jeans jacket and shades, blasting ome psychedelic sitar music, shaggy brown dog ı boat with him. The light here always impresses ıe—the way it glints off the canals—the way it eams thru all the glass windows…

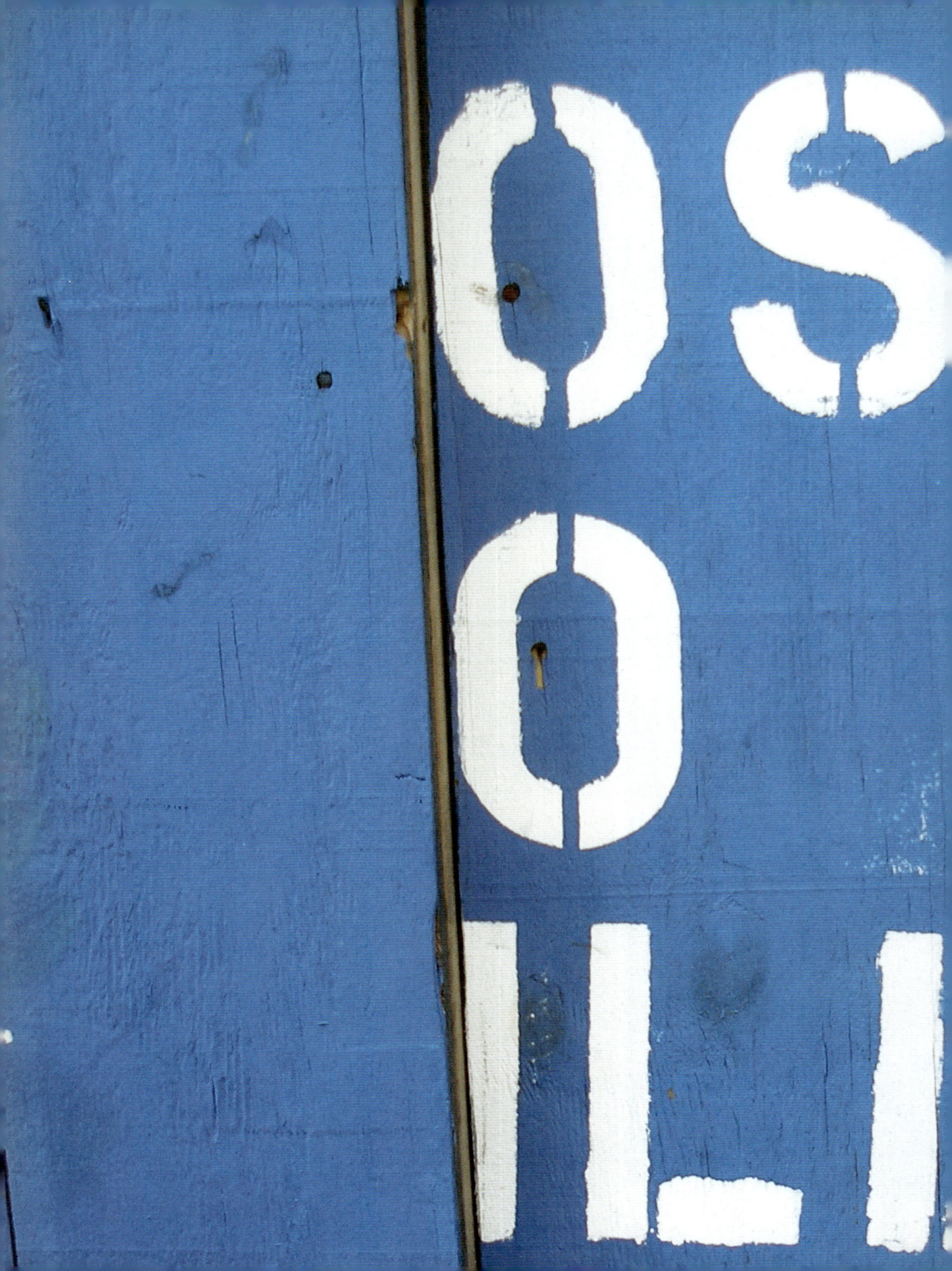

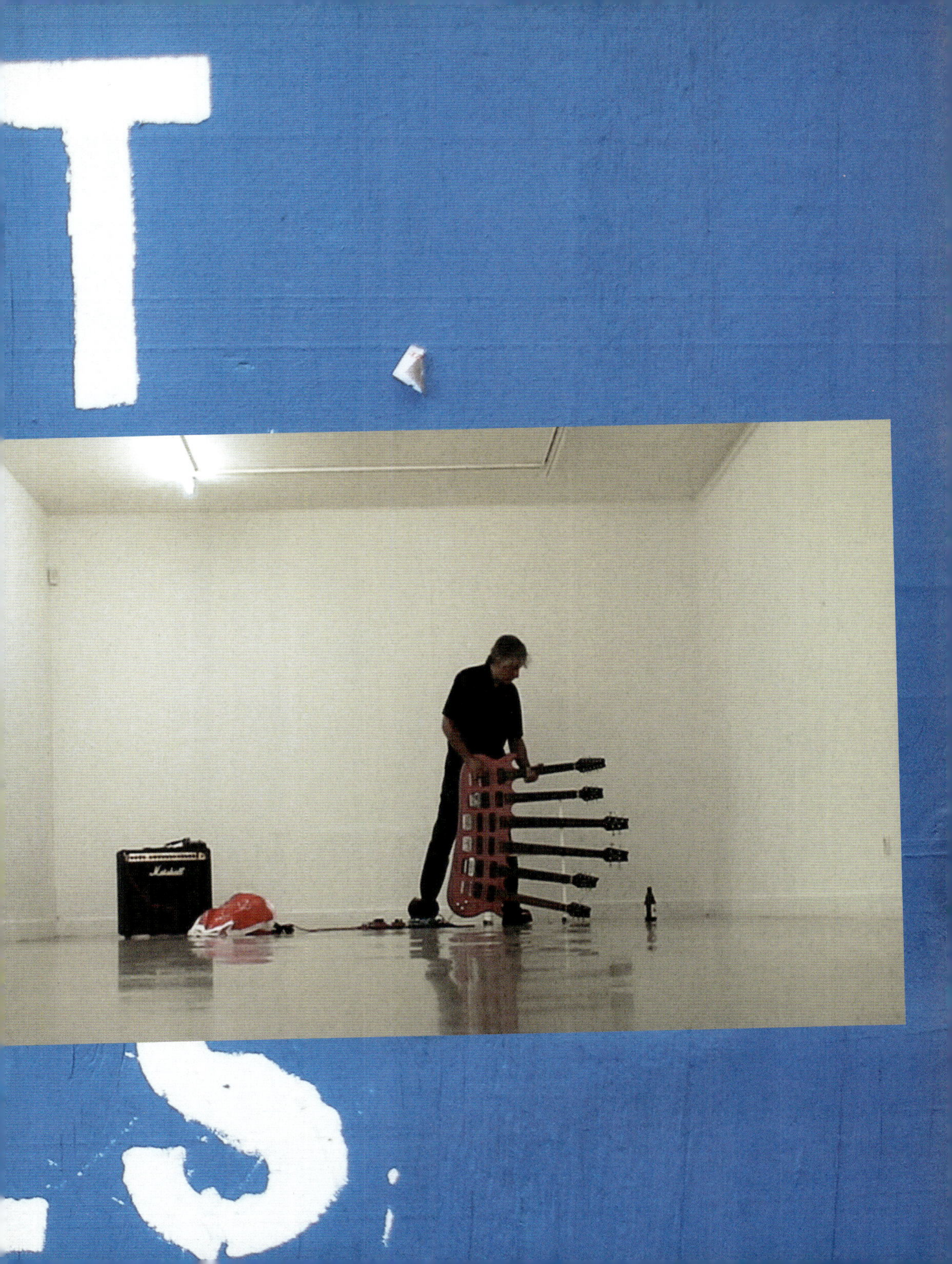

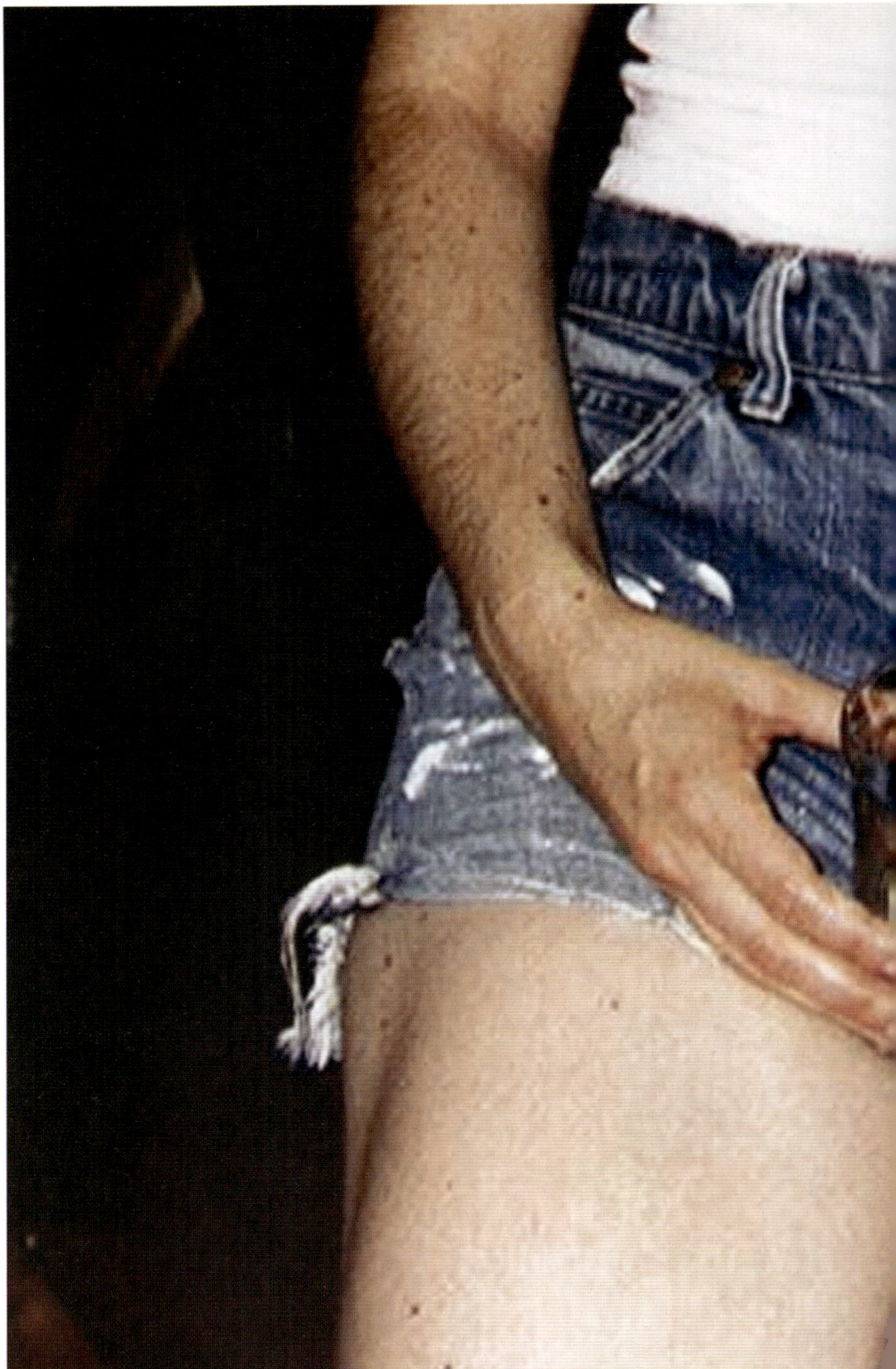

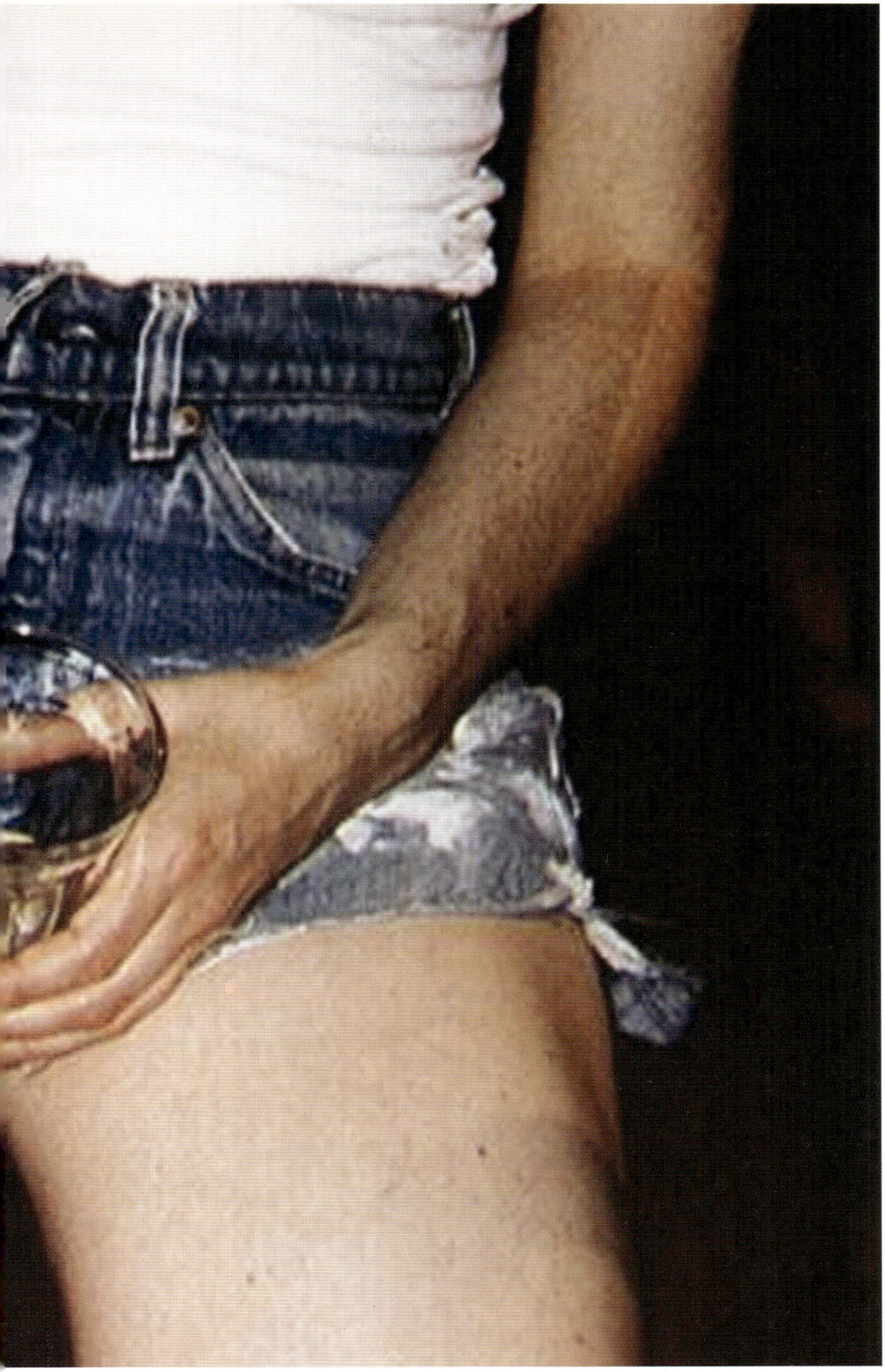

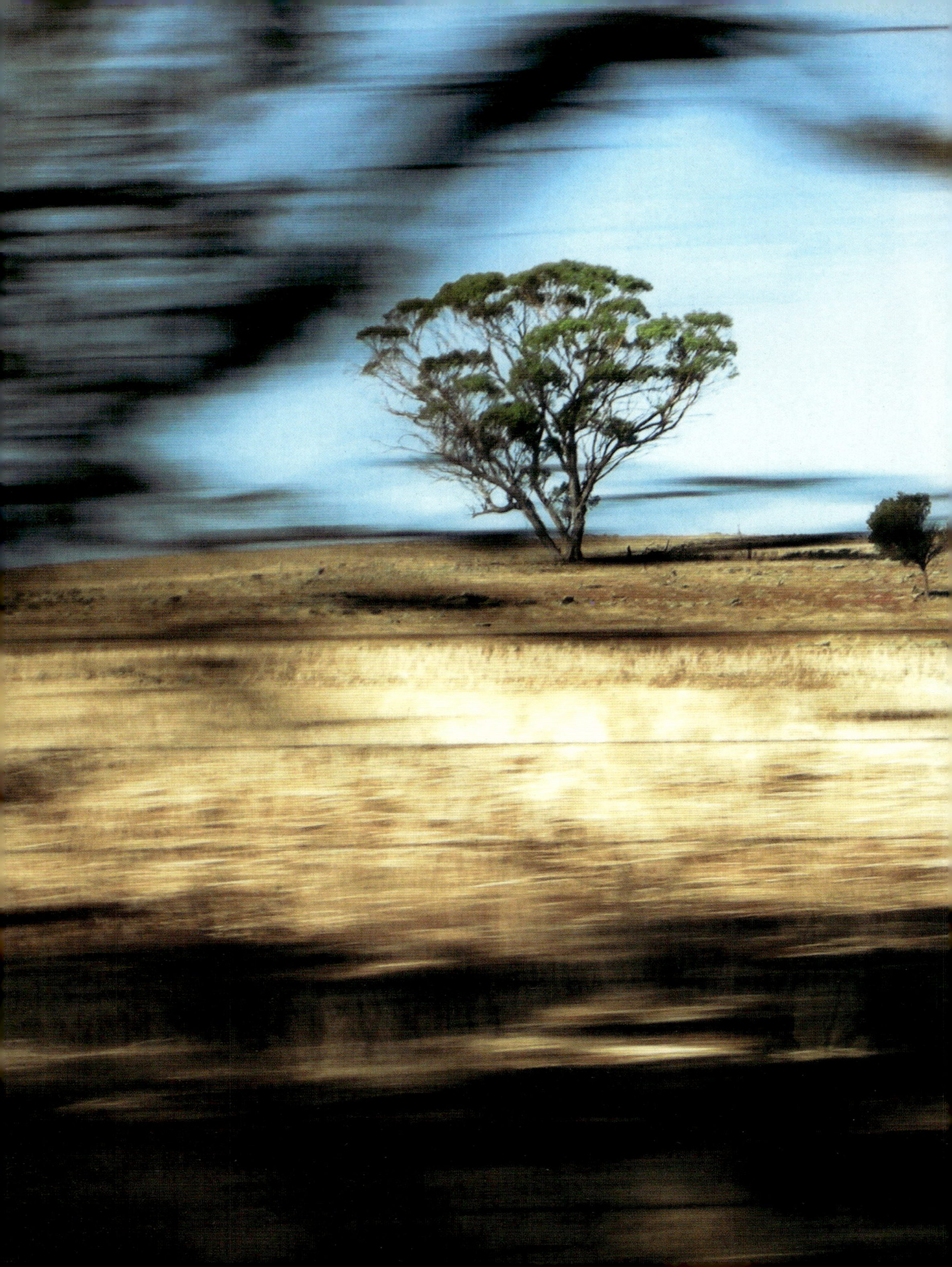

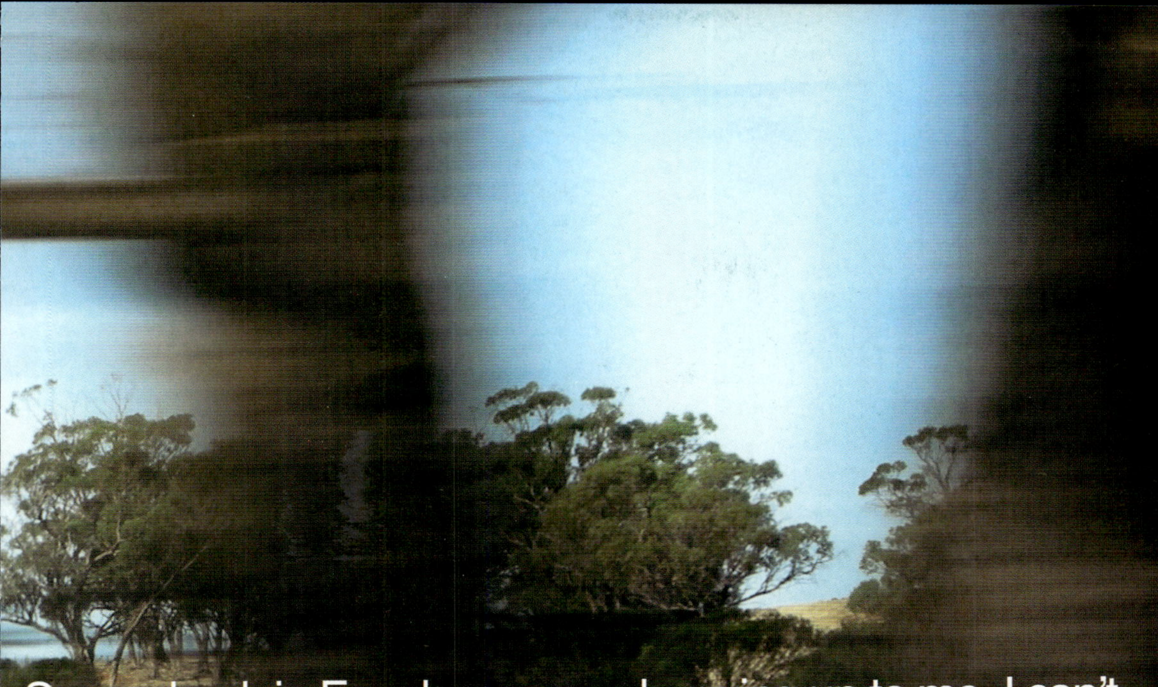

Some drunk in Freo bar comes hurrying up to me, I can't tell what he's getting at. He has something to give me, but he doesn't have it. Can I wait while he goes runs to get it? What is it? Something, he says, slurry and cryptic. Taxi is coming—I've got to get outta here—been out in the salty bush all day—marveling at the pink bark of salmon gum trees and the 28 Parrots dragging the car, and shot gun shells; afraid of Coffin Cheaters cycle gangs but loving the golden landscape of Aussie cut wheatfields lone green trees standing mute on the scorched horizon. It's a record he wants to give me—old fashioned vinyl he wants me to carry out. I know nothing about the hard ice or feet out from under a glancing blow. It's dry and hot here, even in darkness. I've gotta go—taxi is here—moon is bright on clouds, water glinting and mysterious below me. I'll call you from LA the minute we touch down, and expect to hear yr sweet voice. After that I'll tell you everything then we'll keep talking and never stop.

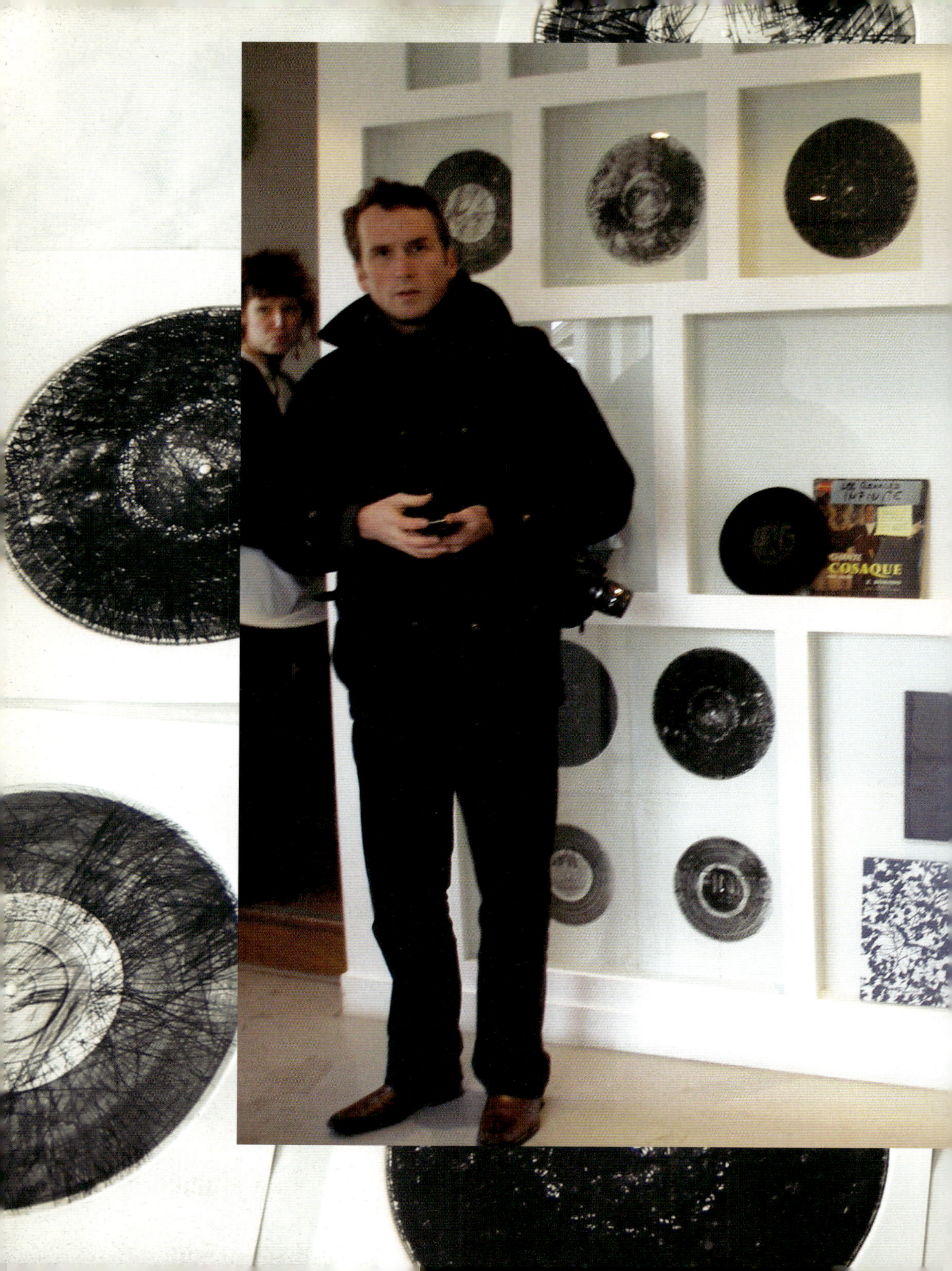
COSAQUE

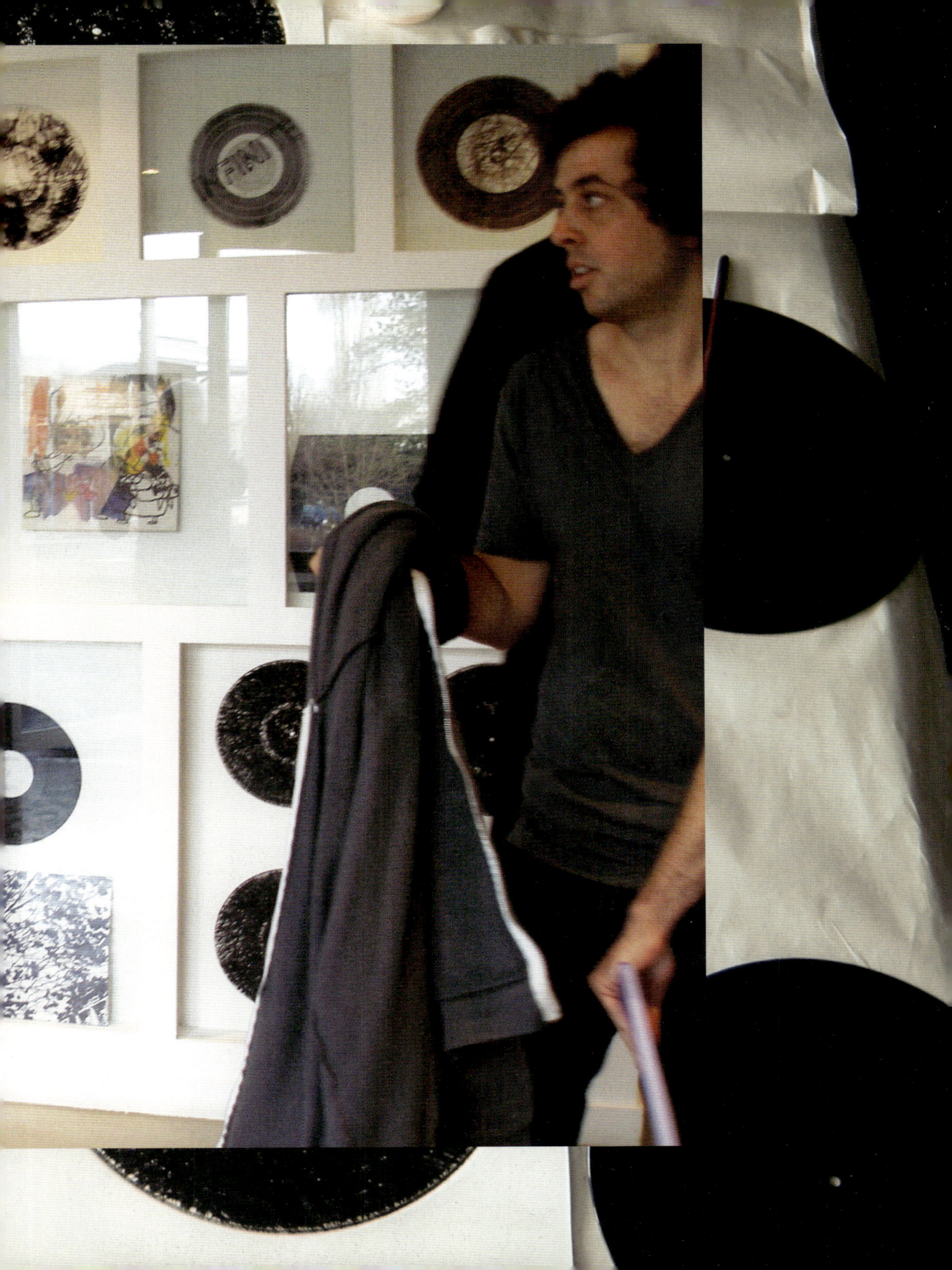

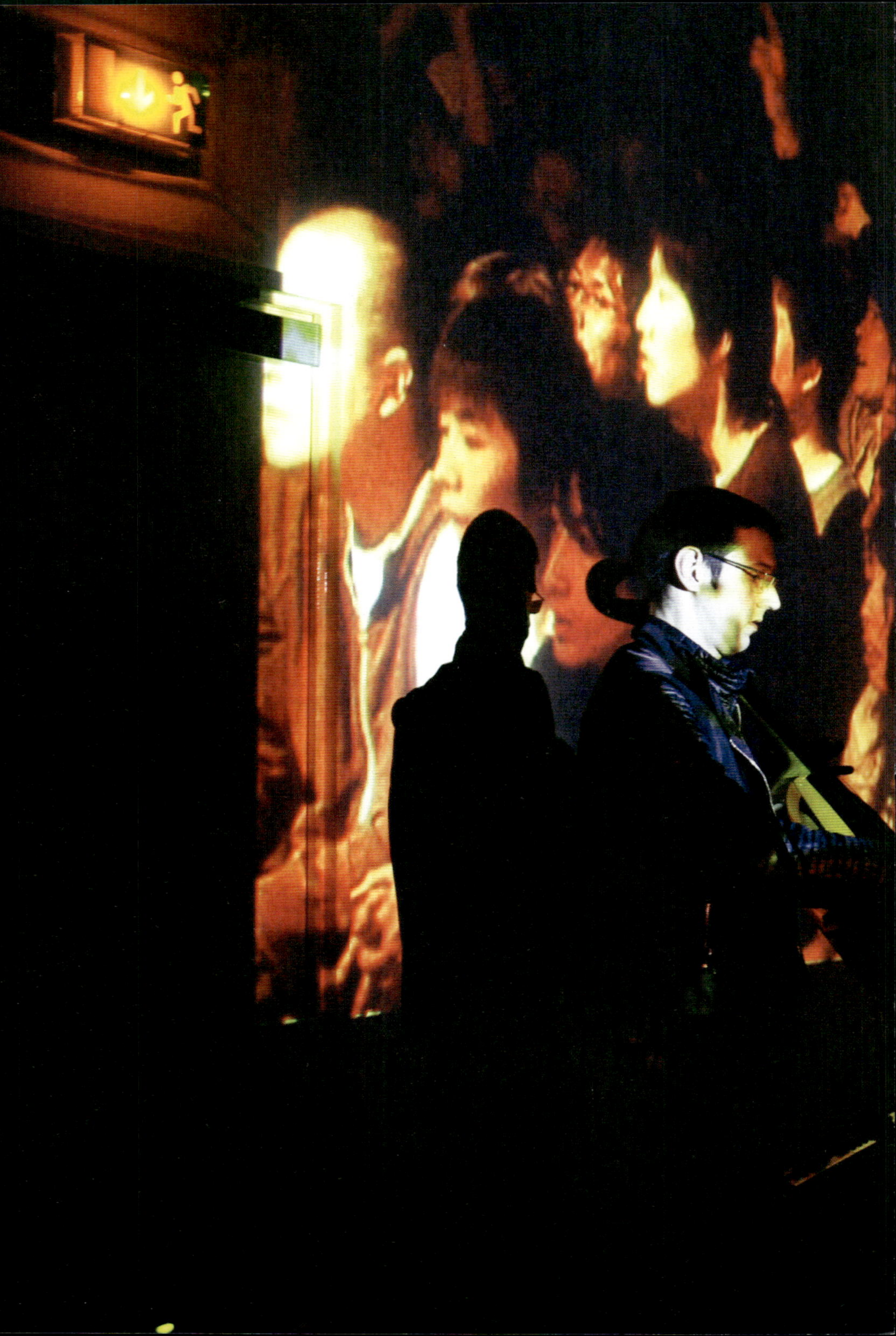

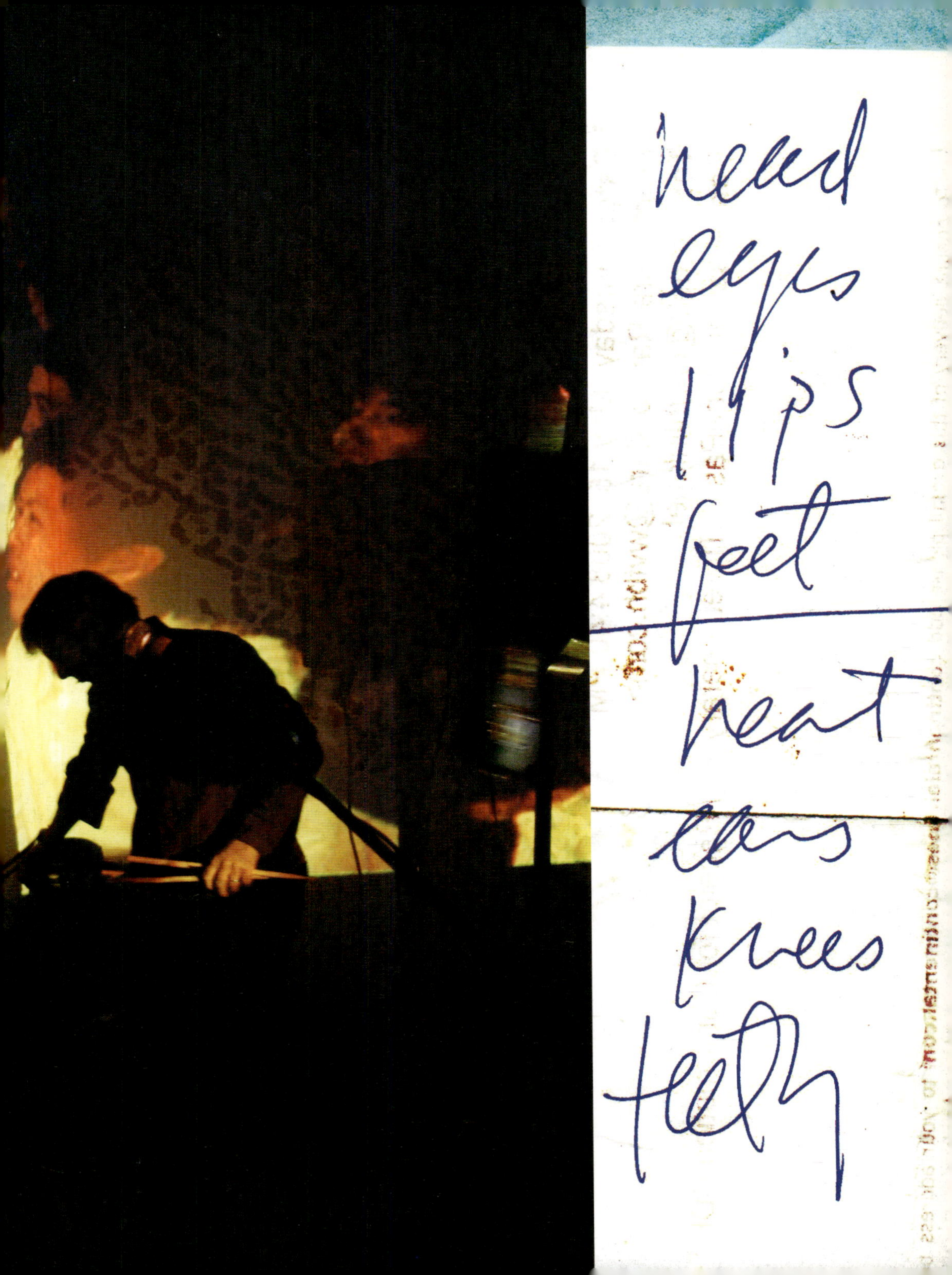
head
eyes
lips
feet
heat
ears
knees
teeth

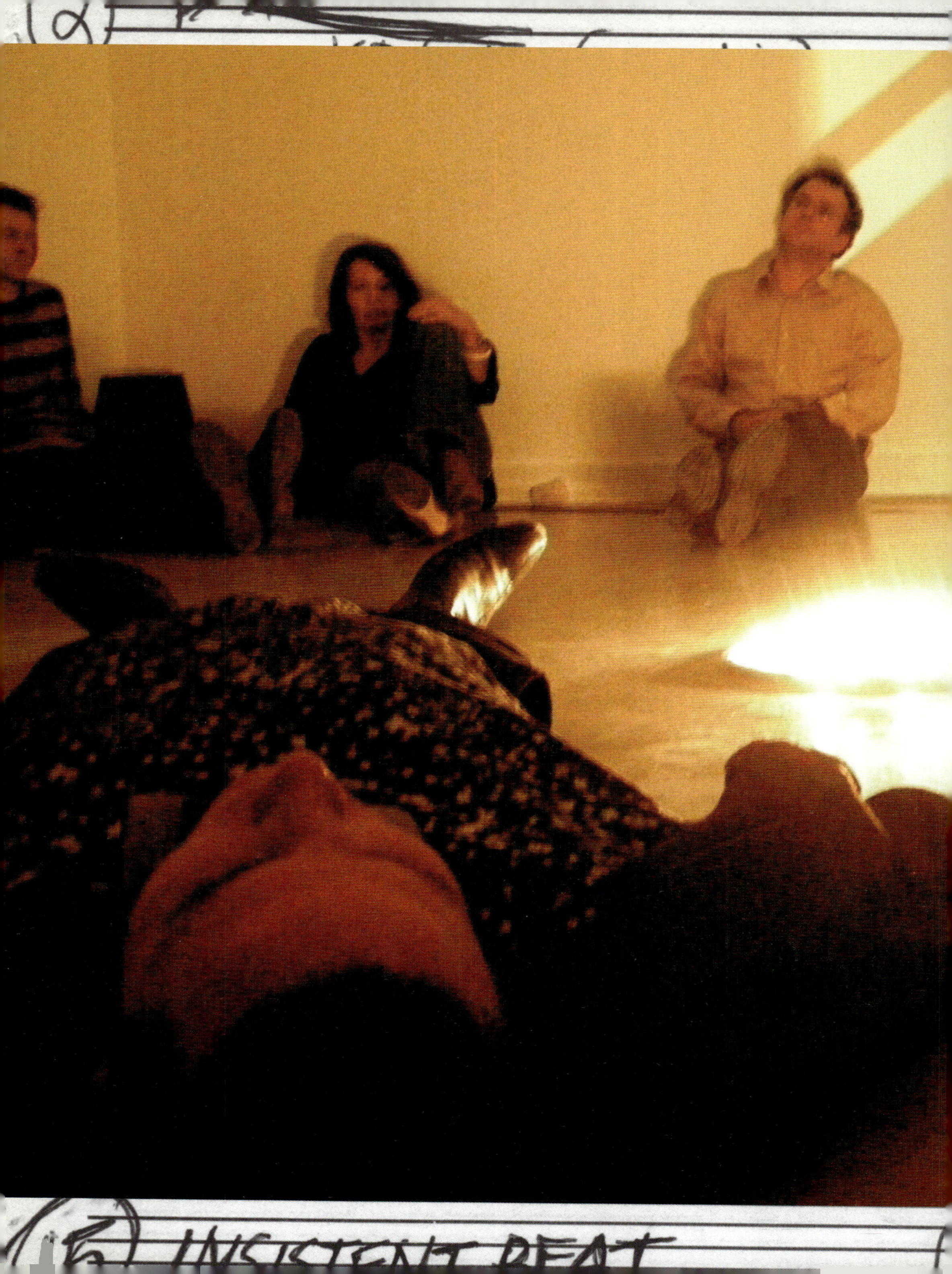

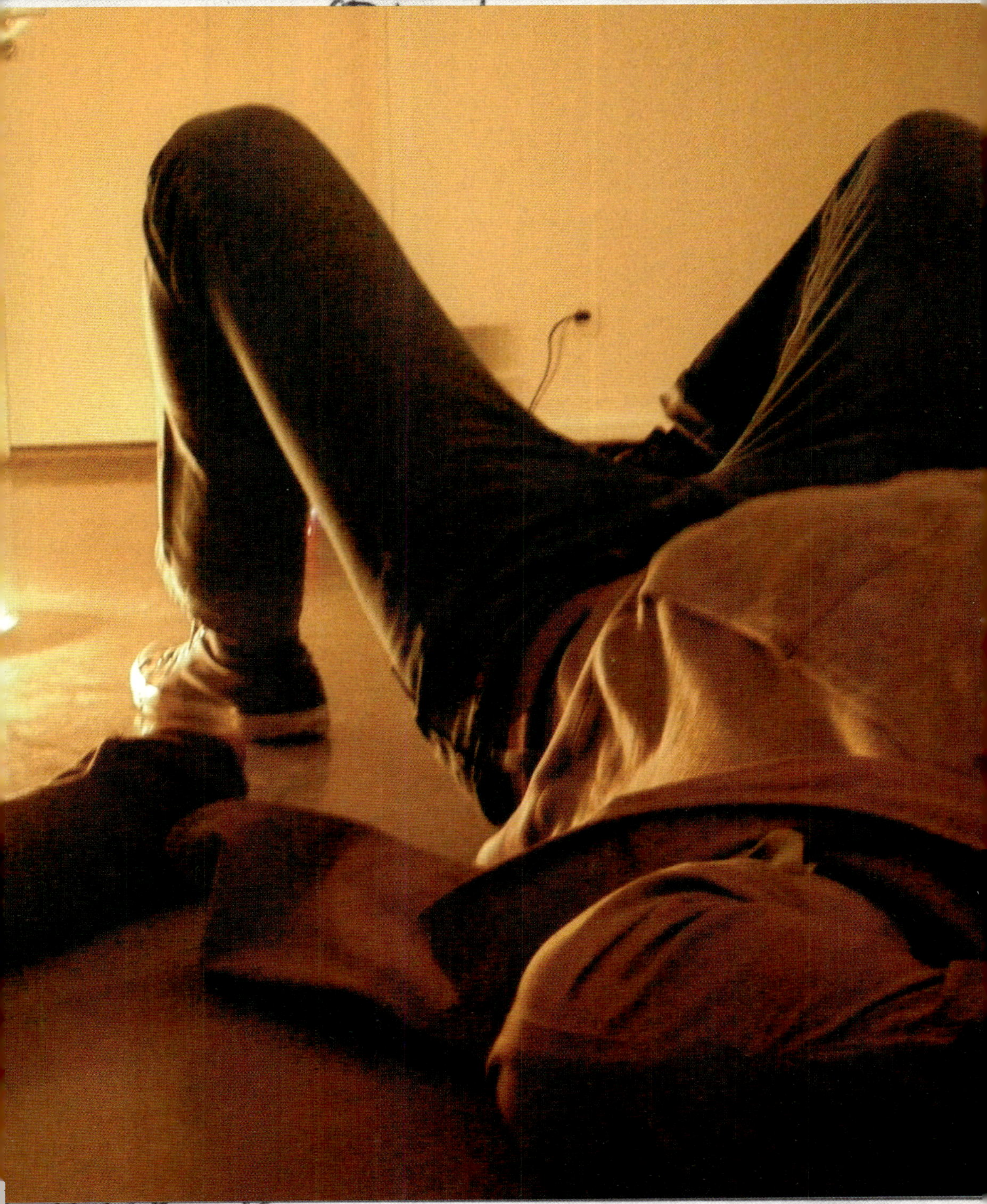

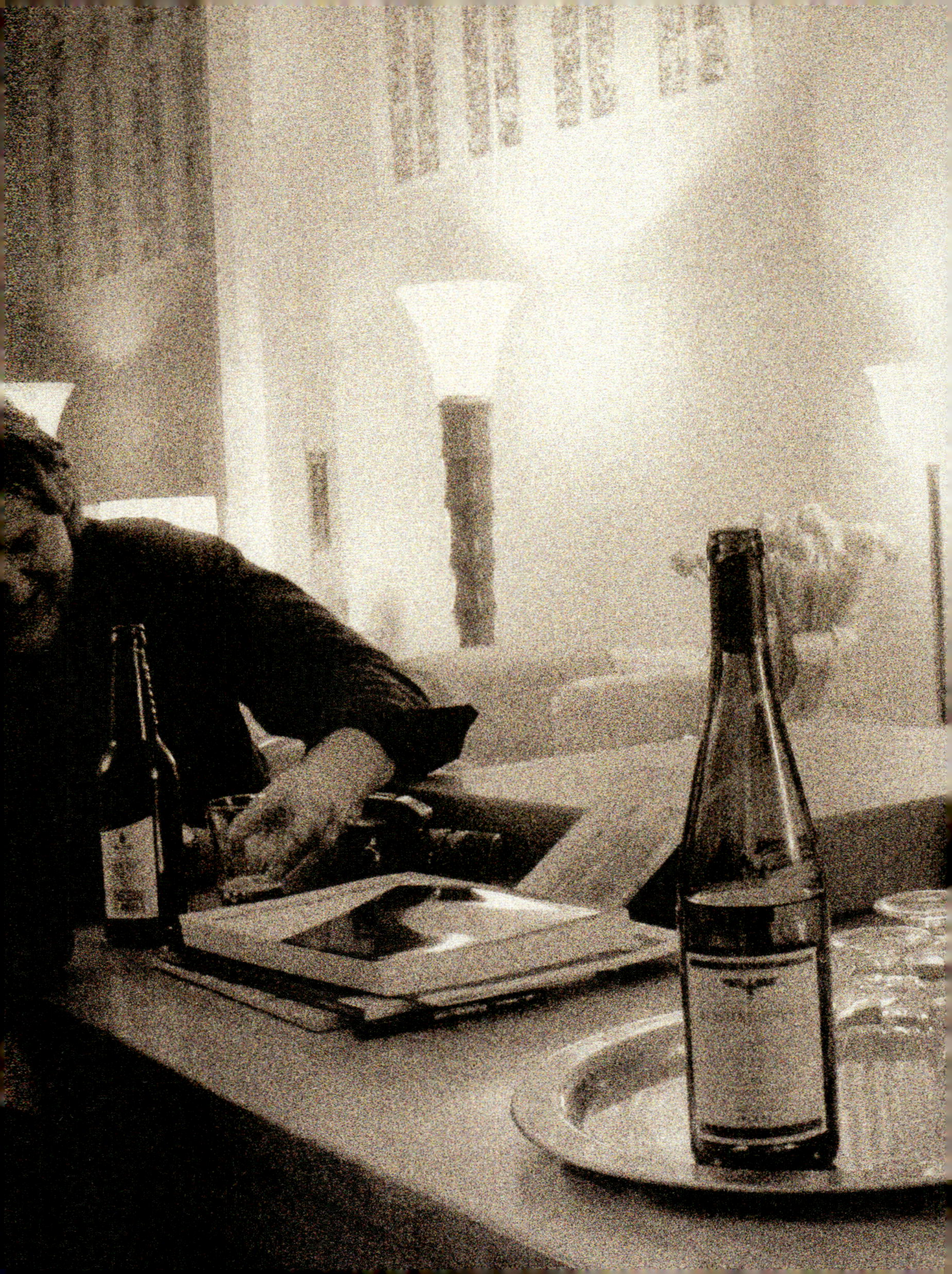

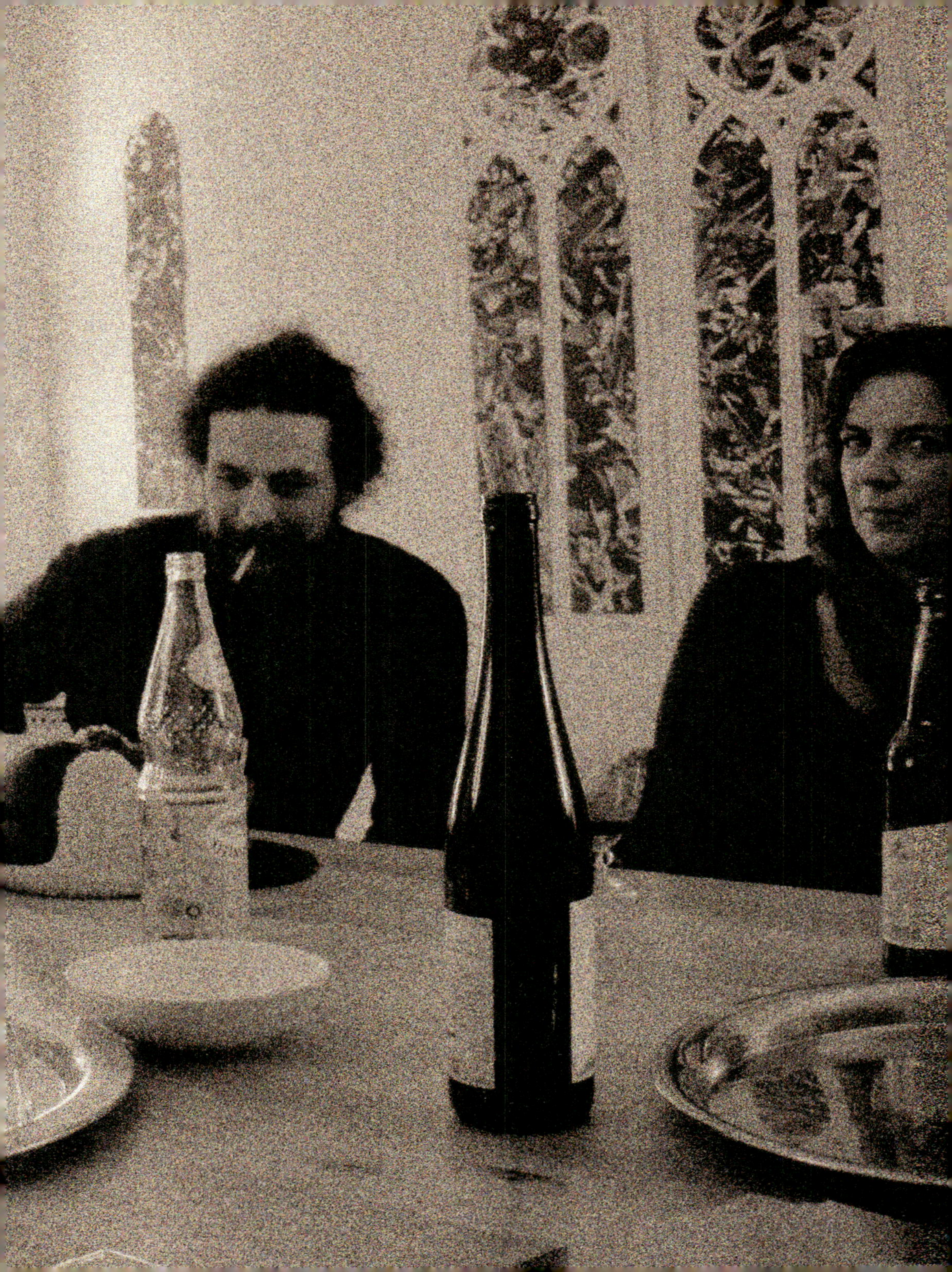

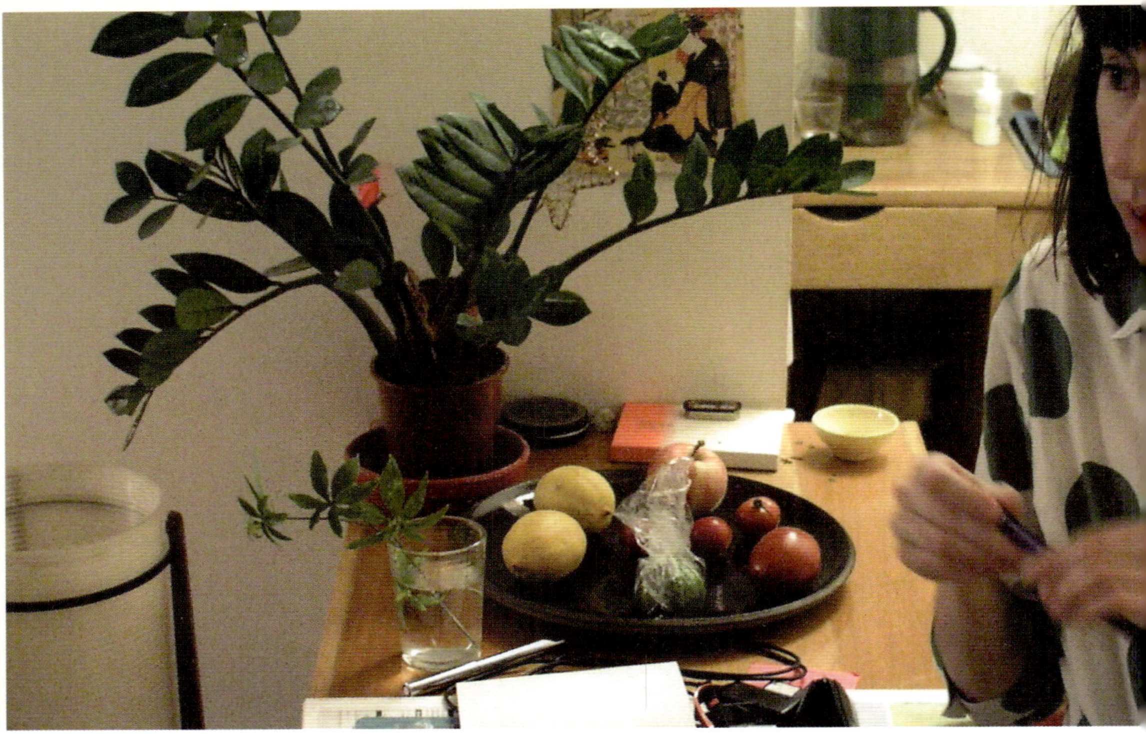

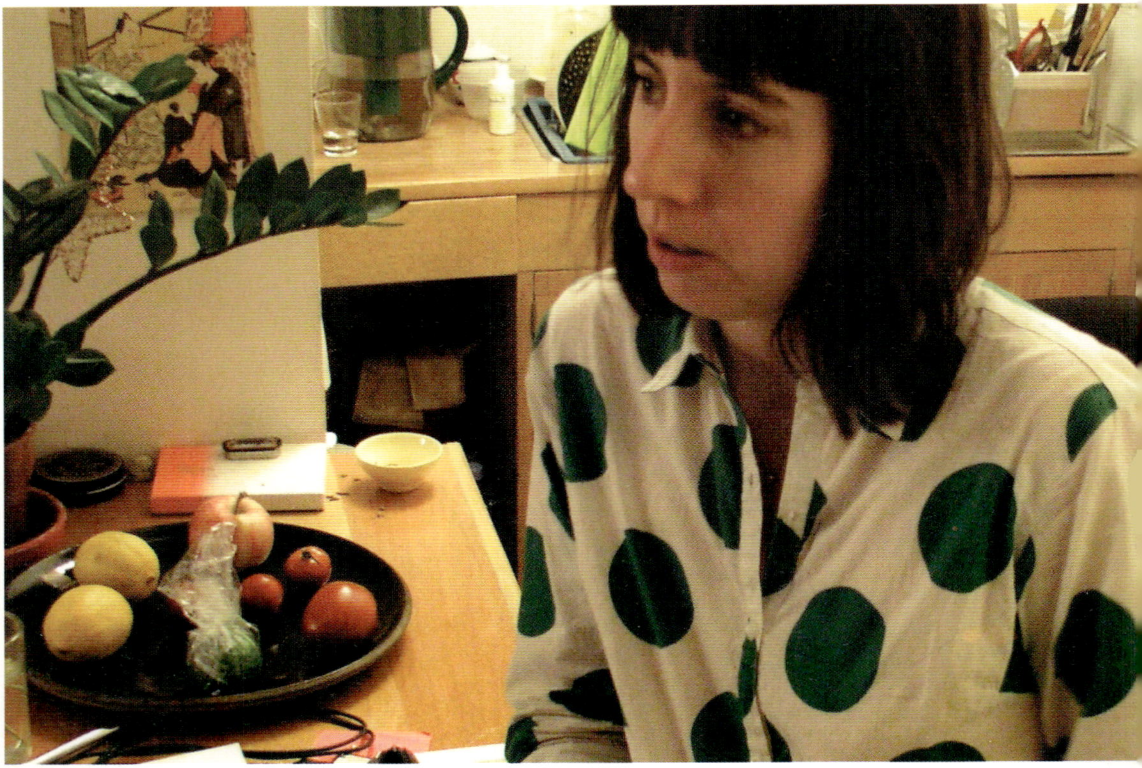

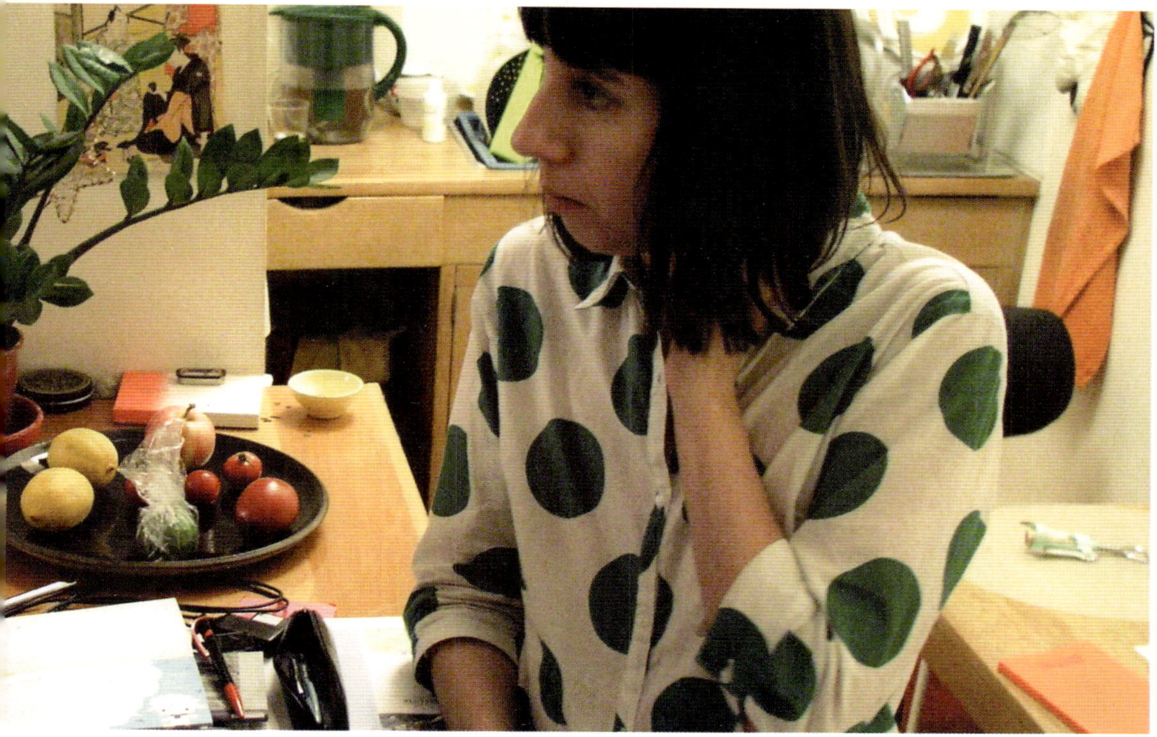

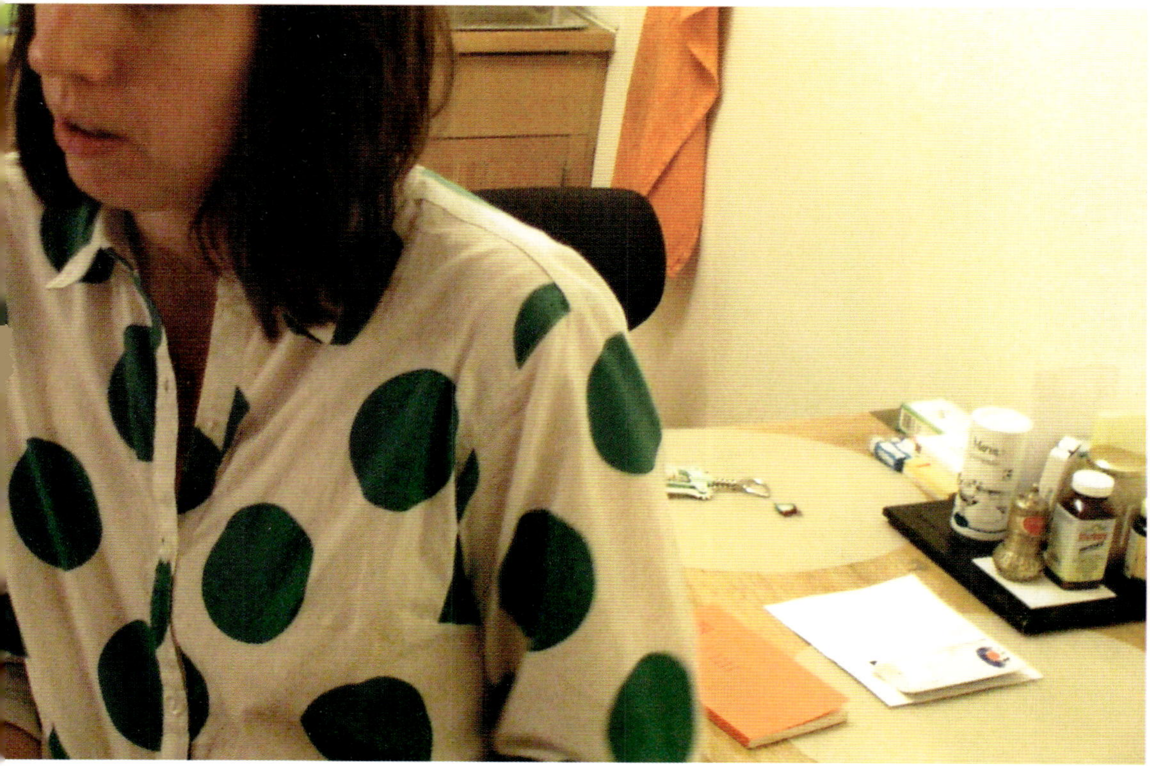

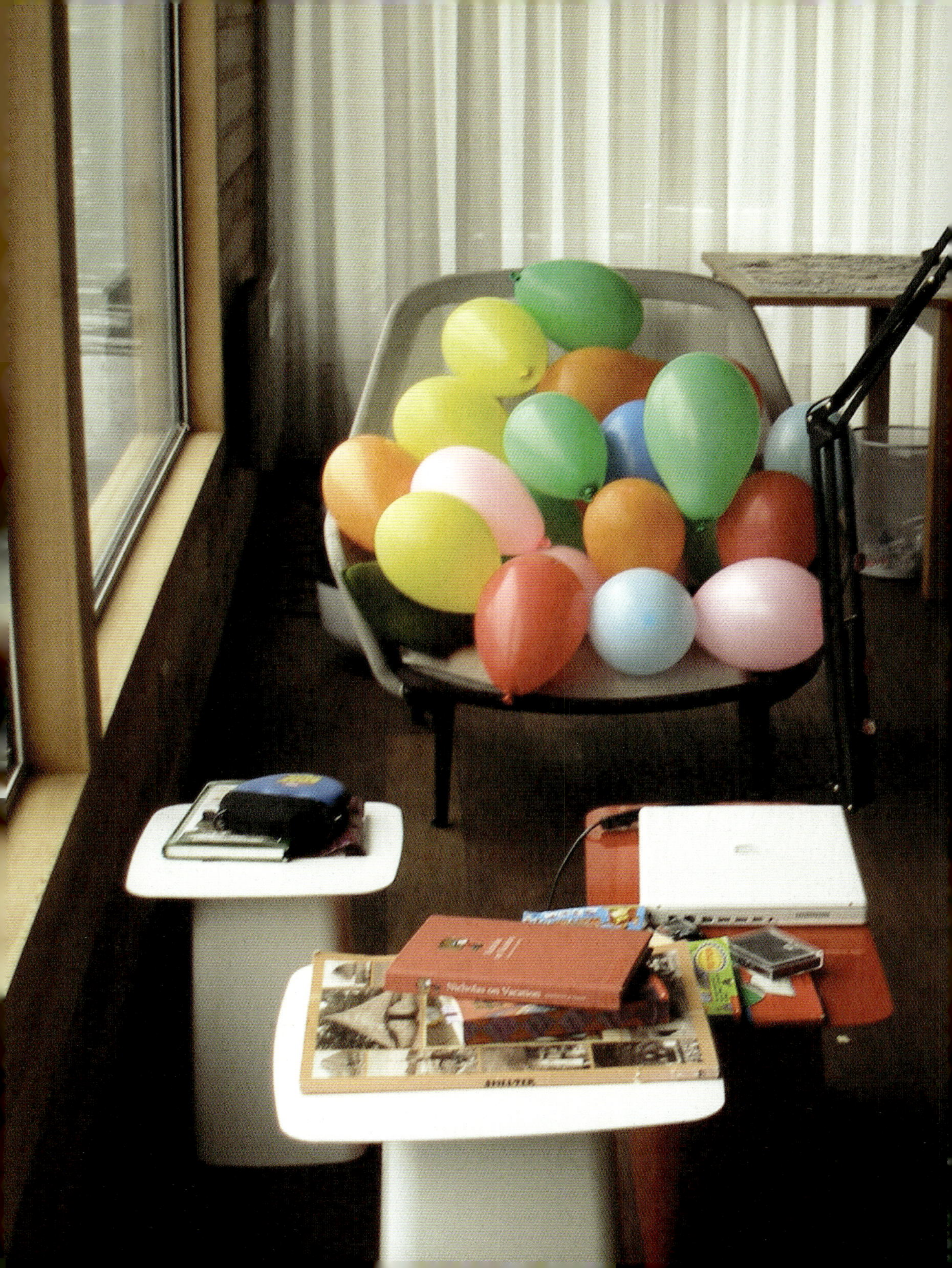
Nicholas on Vacation

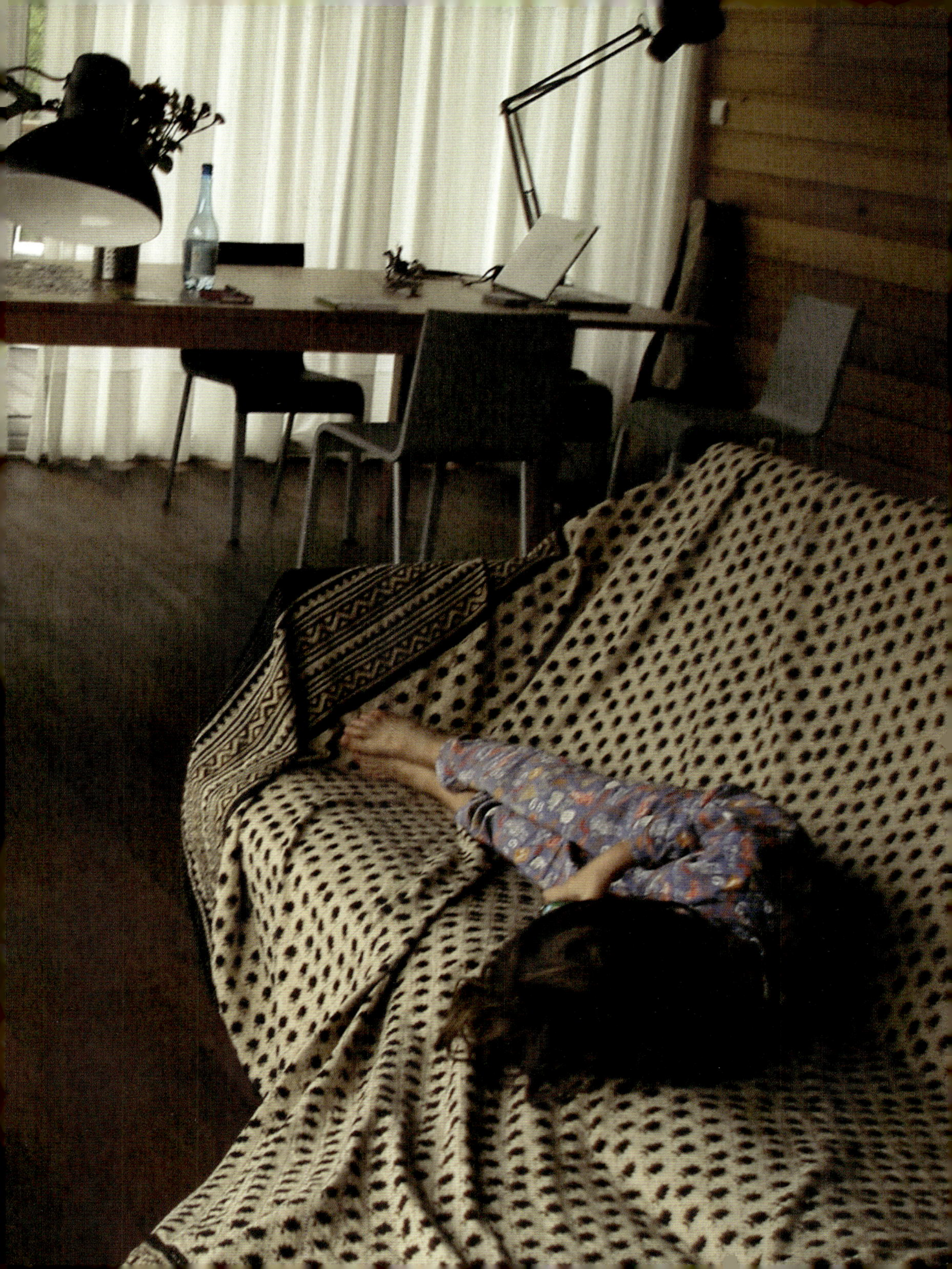

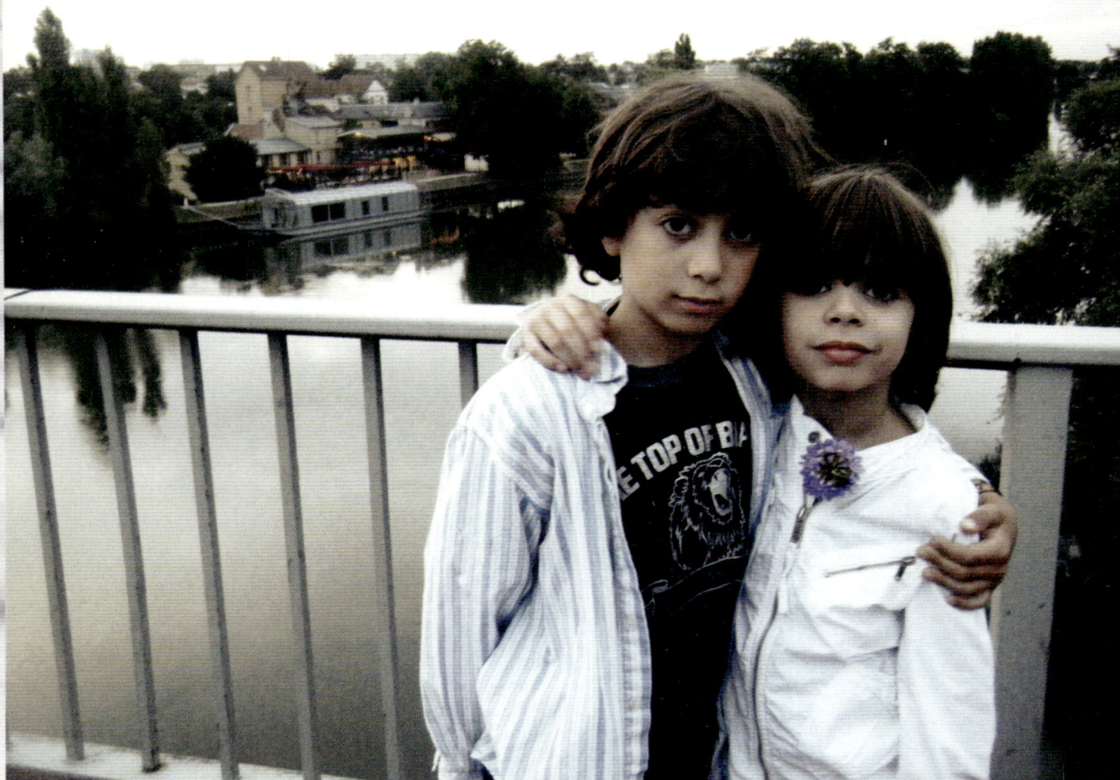

"You get involved in these big

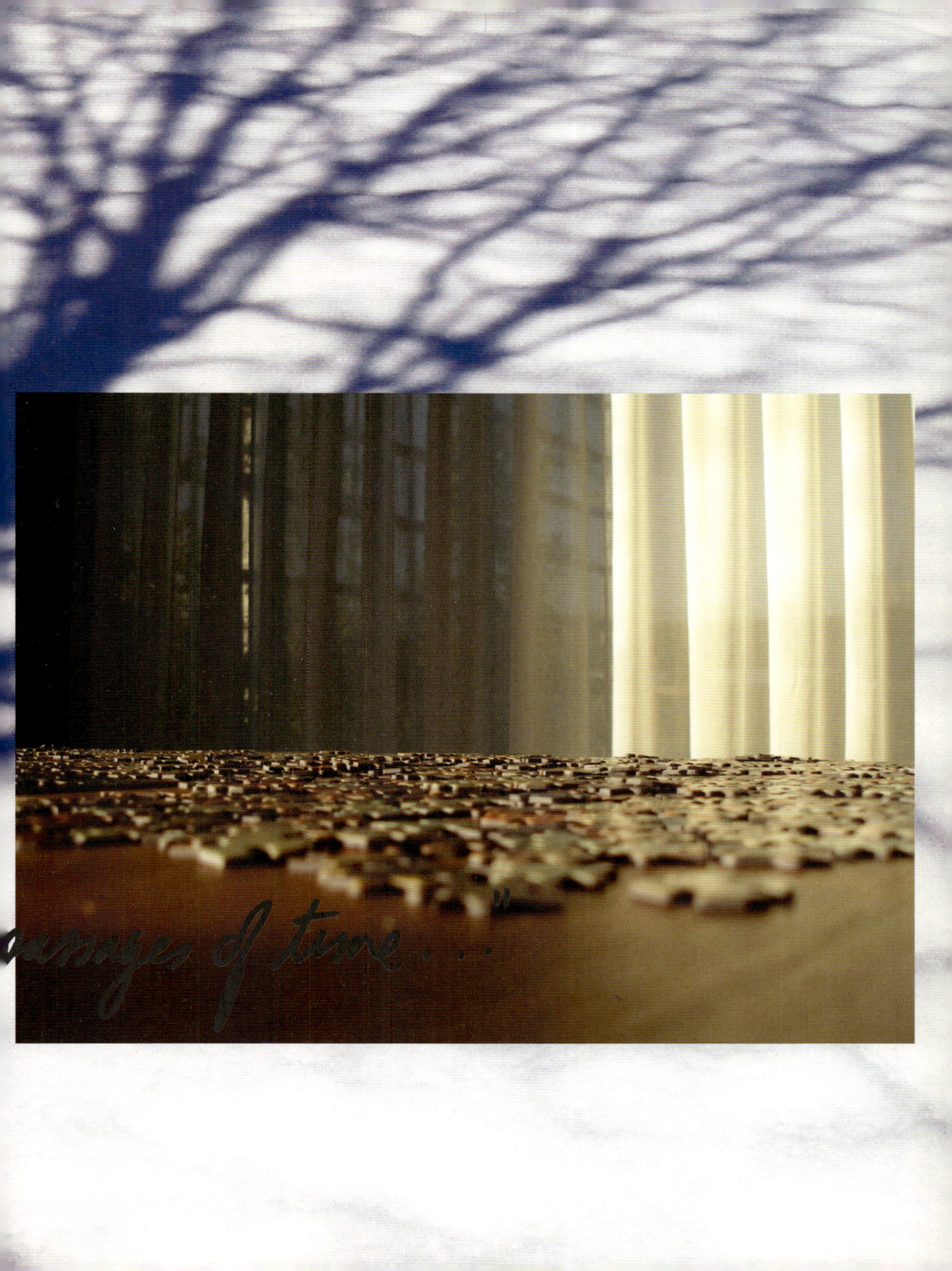
assages of time . . ."

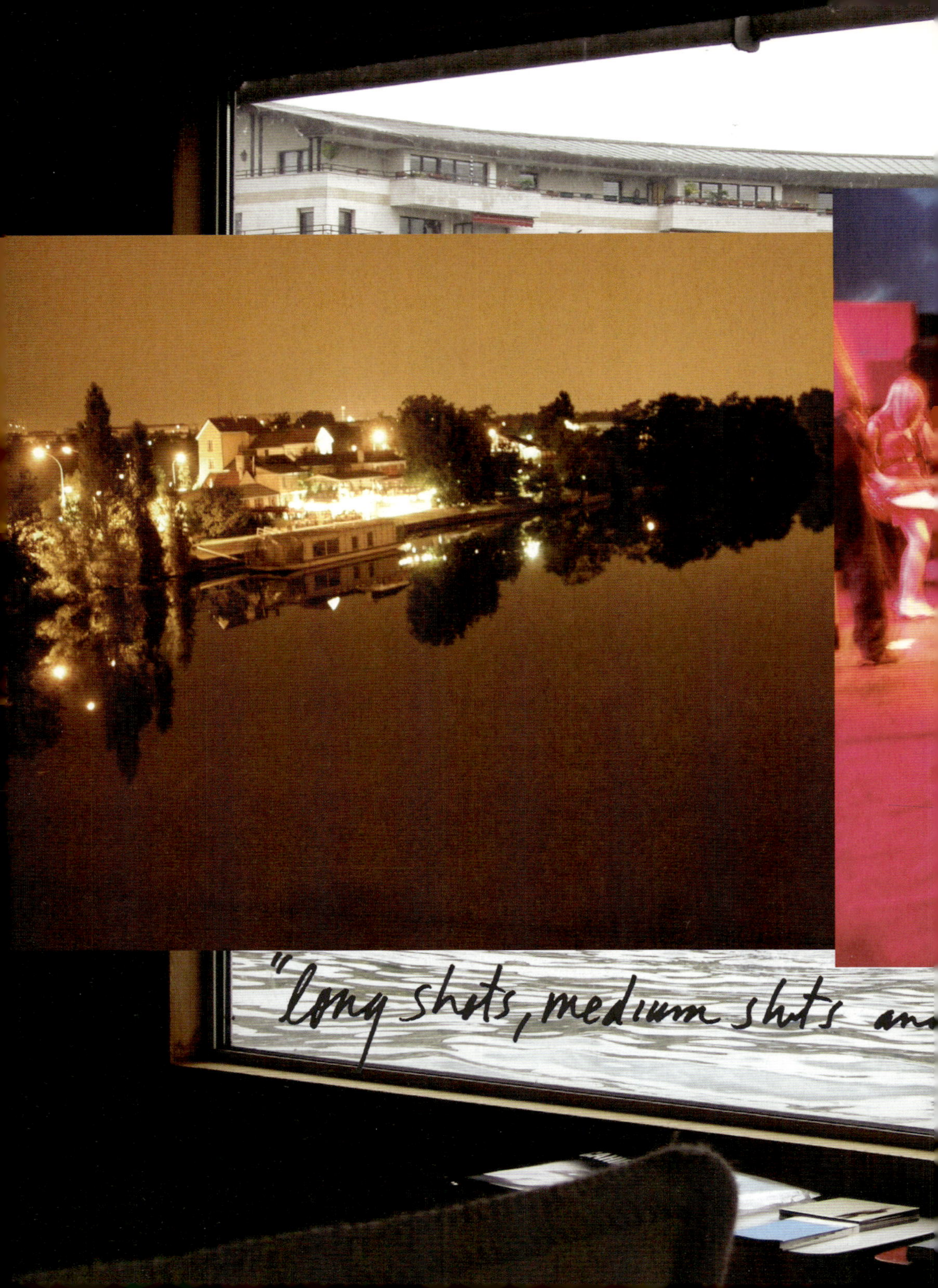
"long shots, medium shots

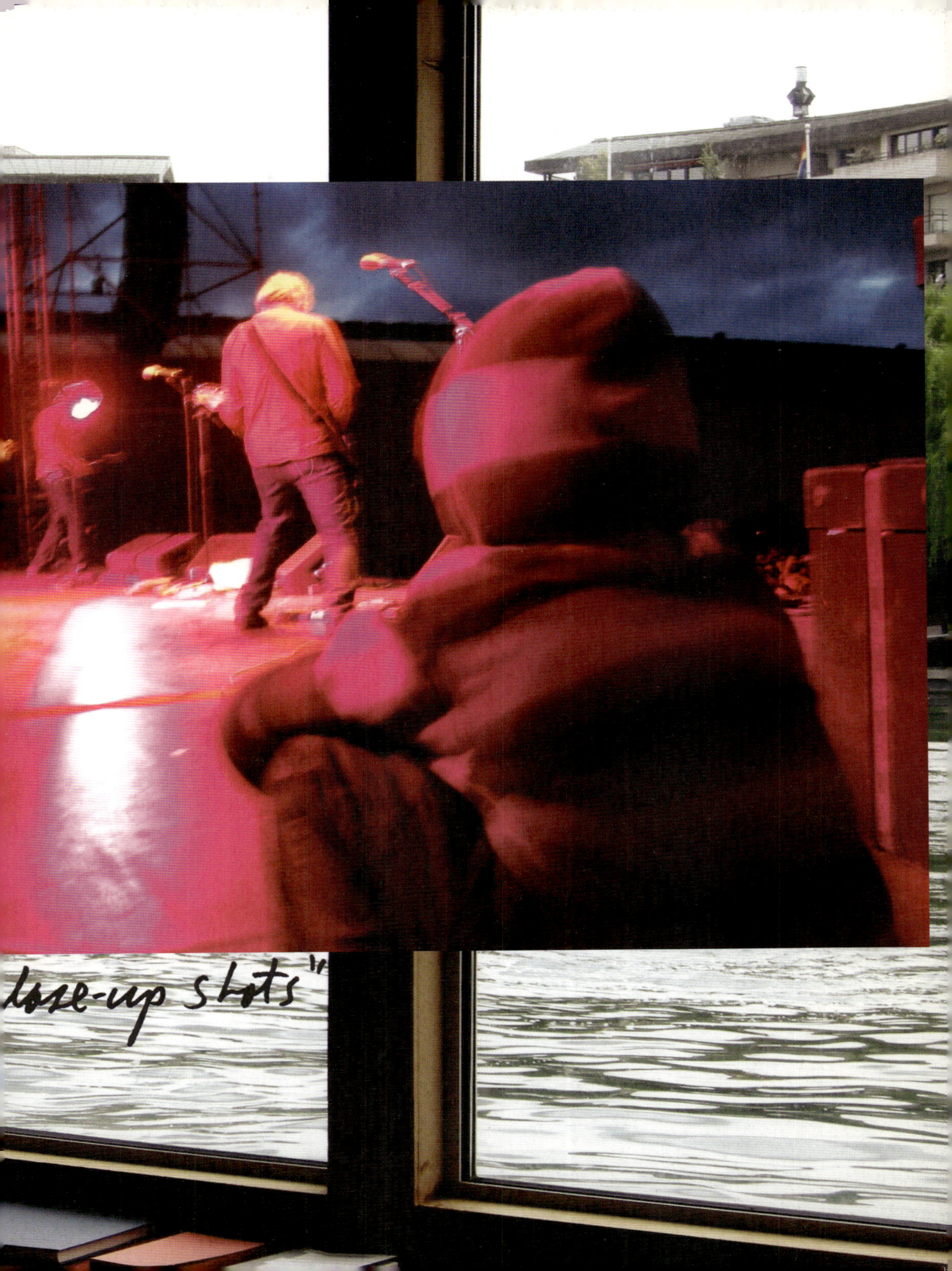
lose-up shots"

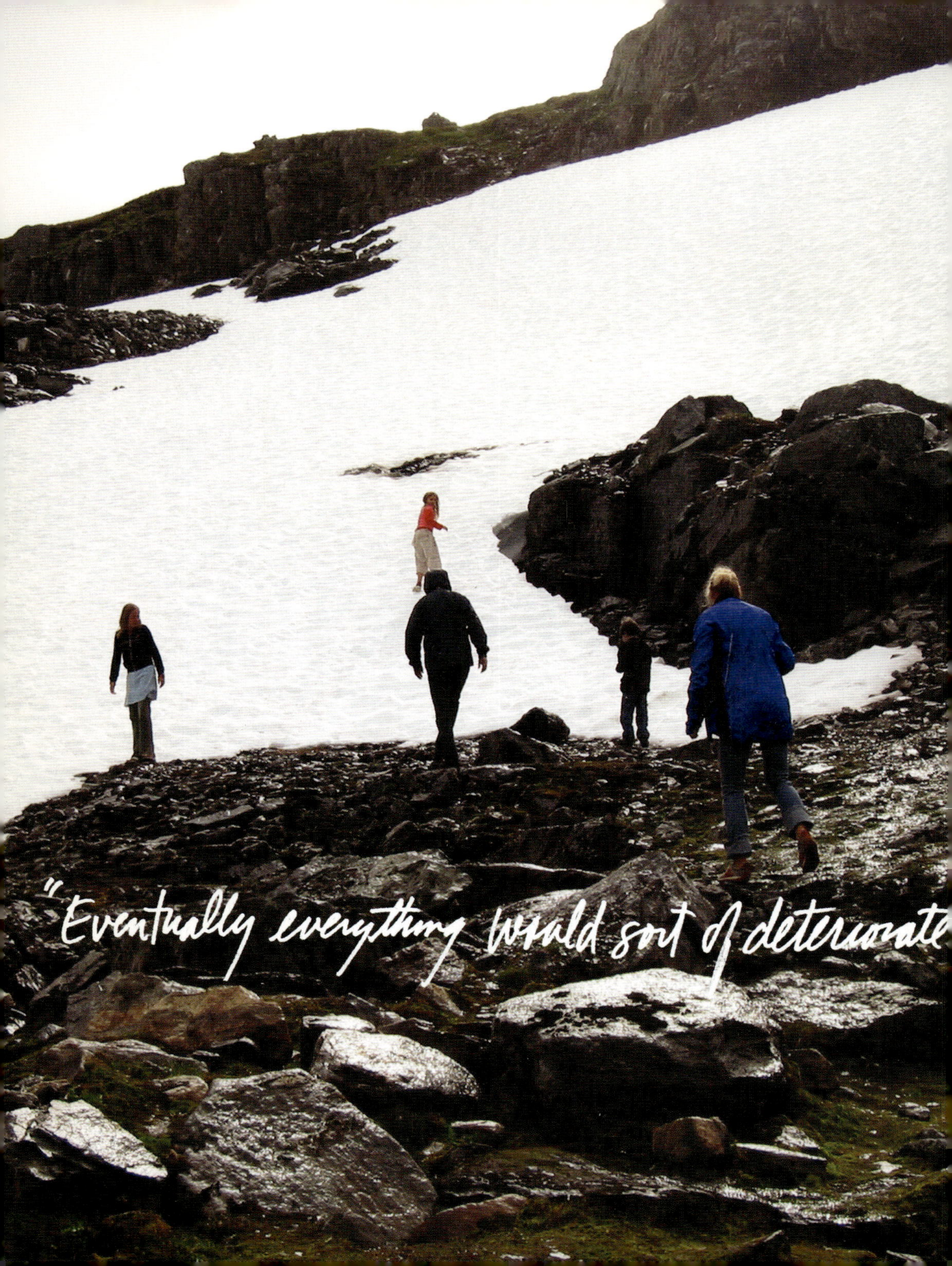
"Eventually everything would sort of deteriorate

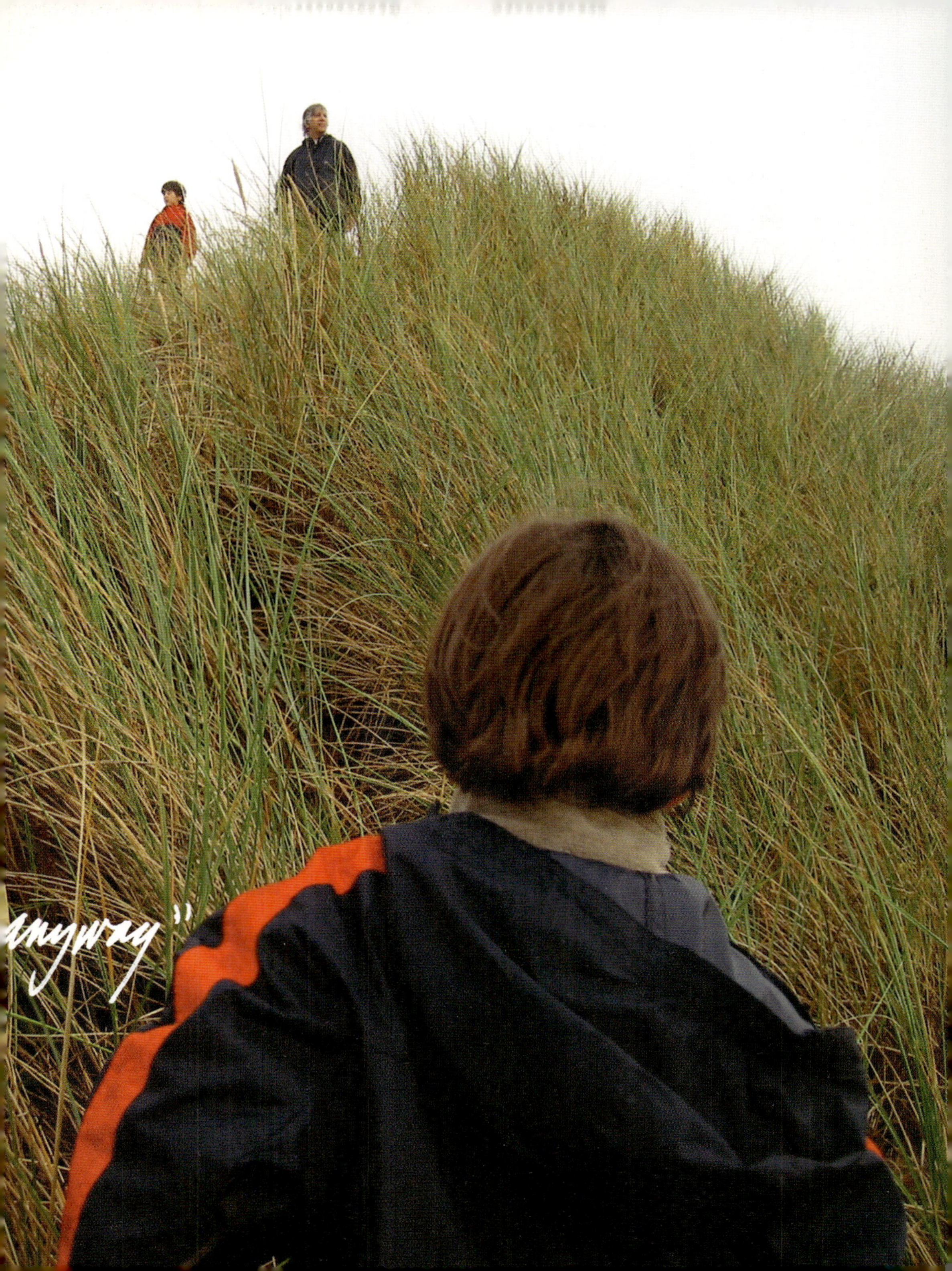
anyway"

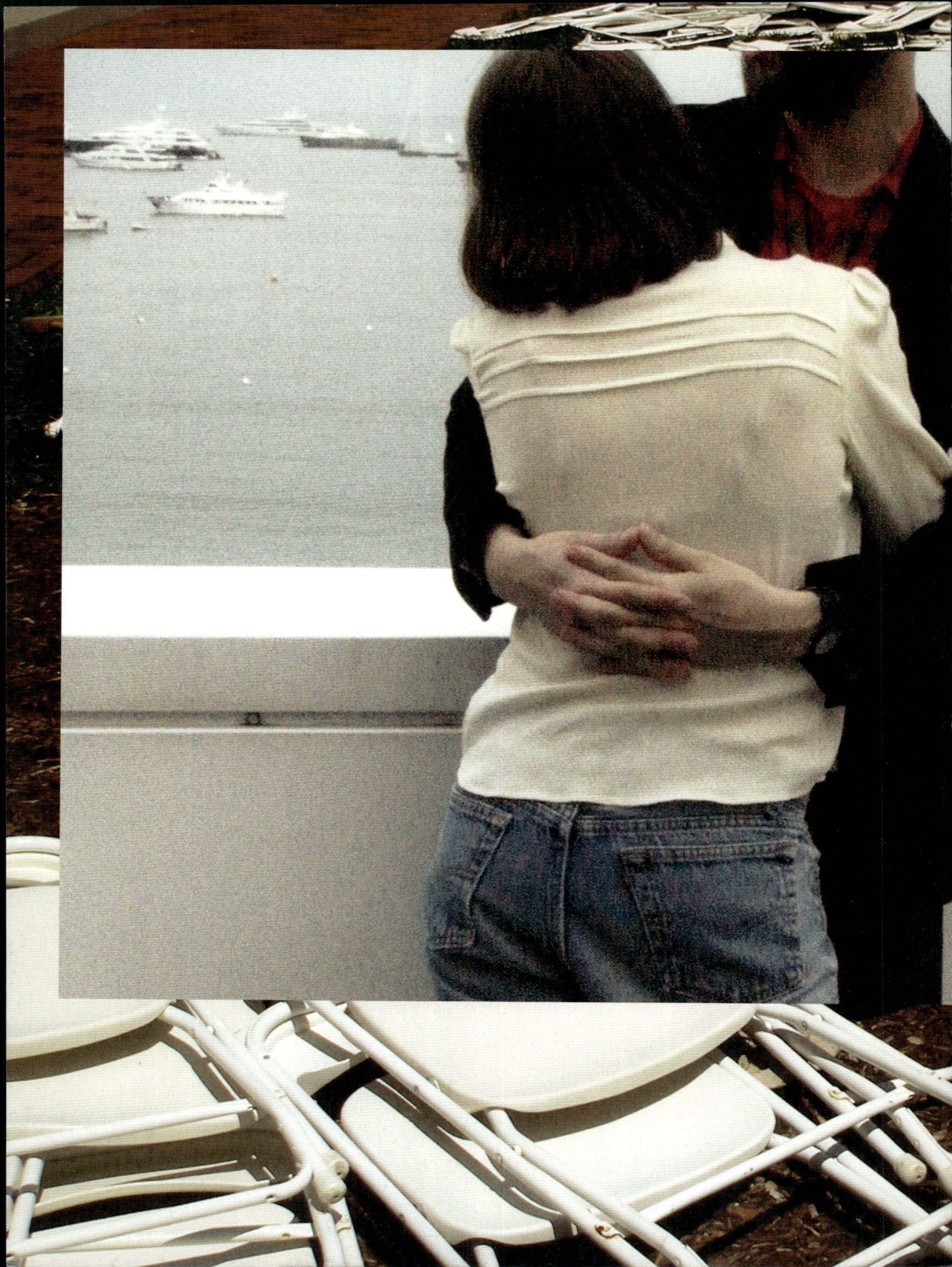

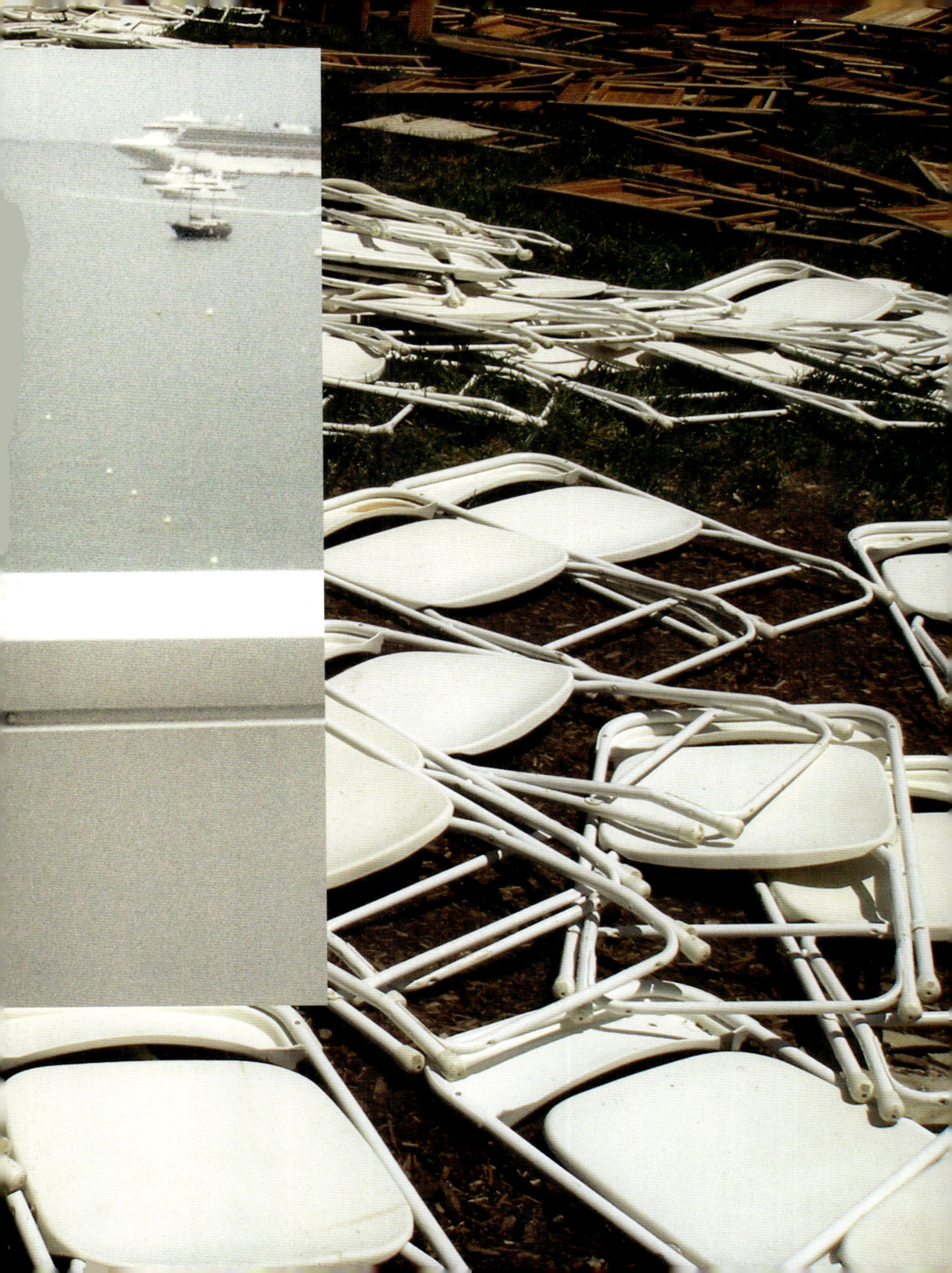

WATER DAYS / JOURS D'EAU

LEAH SINGER • LEE RANALDO

Running time : 45 minutes

The sound work 'Water Days' was realized with the assistance of l'Atelier de Création Radiophonique (ACR), France Culture.

Most sounds recorded in Chatou, France and New York City, 2008 by Lee Ranaldo.
Mixed at Echo Canyon West, NJ.
Balance engineer: Aaron Mullan.
French 'Water Days' voices recorded at Atelier Creation Radiophonique, Paris, by Gilles Mardirossian.
Voices: Laure Salmona, Isabel Leyo, Carson McCullers, Robert Smithson, Lee Ranaldo. 'Water Days' voices: Raphaëlle Gitlis & Leah Singer, Christophe Sauger & Lee Ranaldo.

Thank you: Sylvie Boulanger, Daniel Kurjakovic, Agnes b, Danièle Rivière; Vincent Romagny, Anne-Laure Sacriste, Laure Salmona, Christine Campion, Sebastien Ruiz, Jean-Baptiste Caron, Sandra Doublet, Marie-Dolma Chophel and everyone at Centre national de l'édition et de l'art imprimé, Chatou; Jacob Fabricius; Frank Smith and Gilles Mardirossian at Radio France Culture, Paris; A Constructed World (Jacqui Riva & Geoff Lowe) for the electric guitar; Philippe Langlois; Jan Van Woensel; Richard Julin, Magasin 3, Stockholm; Tara Fracalossi & Thom Lail, HVCC Gallery, Troy NY; Roland Groenenboom, Mona Weiner, Severine Superheights, Jeff Guess, Cameron Jamie, David Shrigley, Brigitte Fontaine & Areski Belkacem, Rhys Chatham, John Giorno, Samon Takahashi, Elein Fleiss, Z Behl, Franck Leibovici, Rik Bas Backer, Maison Martin Margiela, Pip Chodorov, Xavier Garcia Bardon, Josh & Benny Safdie, Eleonore Hendricks, Cody, Sage & Frey.

WATER DAYS

WATER DAYS is an environmental sound recording, set in motion by two summer residencies which we undertook in August 2007 and 2008 at the Centre national de l'édition et de l'art imprimé (Cneai) in Chatou, just outside of Paris. We were working on prints in the atelier and living on the Maison Flottante; sleeping on the Seine! During our stay we also spent time contemplating and recording the sounds within which we were immersed – the river, boats, birds, winds, waves, even the air over the Seine; local church bells, sounds in the atelier where we were working. To these we added audio recorded in other locales and also voices: artist Robert Smithson, writer Carson McCullers, friends and associates. We prepared a text together, which forms the center section of the audio piece. The voices and conversations around us were in both English and French; both found their way into the final version of the audio piece, commissioned by Atelier Creation Radiophonique, France. Finally, sounds recorded in the Cneai gallery space in August 2008 on a very strange and special electric guitar (6 necks on it!) which was on exhibit at Cneai as part of a show by A Constructed World (Jacqui Riva & Geoff Lowe) – loud, vibrating sounds, bouncing around inside the galleries of Cneai while the sun shone and a wedding party gathered outside, were woven in and out and around these recordings.

LEAH SINGER • LEE RANALDO
NYC October 2009

Printed by
DZS GRAFIK
SLOVENIA
EUROPE

February 2010